LET'S SIGN for Work: BSL Guide for Service Providers
2nd Revised Edition

FROM CO-SIGN COMMUNICATIONS (inc DeafBooks.co.uk)

Some established items marked (POD) have been moved to
PRINT ON DEMAND from www.Amazon.co.uk

LET'S SIGN DICTIONARY EVERYDAY BSL: 2nd Edition Revised & Enlarged

LET'S SIGN POCKET DICTIONARY: BSL Concise Beginner's Guide

SIGNS OF HEALTH: A Pocket Medical Sign Language Guide (BSL)

BSL 100 EVERDAY SIGNS: Beginner's Handbook

OUR SCHOOL SIGNS

LET'S SIGN FAMILY TOPICS: BSL for Children and their Carers

LET'S SIGN & DOWN SYNDROME: Signs for Children with Special Needs

EARLY YEARS

LET'S SIGN EARLY YEARS: BSL Child and Carer Guide **2nd Edition**

LET'S SIGN BSL EARLY YEARS & BABY SIGNS: Poster/Mats A3 Set of 2

LET'S SIGN BSL: EARLY YEARS CURRICULUM TUTOR BOOK & CD (POD)

LET'S SIGN BSL: EARLY YEARS CURRICULUM STUDENT BOOK

FLASHCARDS

LET'S SIGN BSL: Early Years & Baby Signs FLASHCARDS

LET'S SIGN BSL: FEELINGS & EMOTIONS FLASHCARDS

LET'S SIGN BSL : House & Home FLASHCARDS

LET'S SIGN BSL THANK YOU CARDS

LET'S SIGN SCIENCE: BSL Vocabulary for KS 1, 2, & 3 (Dictionary) (POD)

GRAPHICS PACKS
On annual licences for creating your own materials

see www.Widgit.com

LET'S SIGN BSL: Full Adult Dictionary Set Graphics Pack

LET'S SIGN BSL: Baby & Early Years Graphics Pack

LET'S SIGN SCIENCE: BSL (KS 1, 2, & 3) Graphics Pack

Our publications are also available on Kindle and DeafBooks has a growing collection of POD books in bite-sized topics for learners - see back page for details and QR code links to listings.

LET'S SIGN: For Work
A BSL Guide for Service Providers

CATH SMITH
Illustrated by Cath Smith

CO-SIGN COMMUNICATIONS
Incorporating DeafBooks.co.uk

Copyright © 2003 by Cath Smith

The right of Cath Smith to be identified as author of this work has been asserted by her in accordance with the Copyright, Designs and Patents Act 1988.

First published 2003
Reprinted 2004, 2005, 2006
2nd Edition (Revised and enlarged) 2007
Reprinted 2019, 2022, 2023, 2025

ISBN-10: 1-905913-03-6
ISBN-13: 978-1-905913-03-9

All rights reserved. No part of this publication may be reproduced, stored in a retrieval system, or transmitted, in any form or by any means, electronic, mechanical, photocopying, recording or otherwise without the prior permission of the Copyright owner.

Published by Co-Sign Communications
Incorporating DeafBooks
Stockton-on-Tees TS18 5HH
Tel: 01642 580505
info@letssign.co.uk - info@deafbooks.co.uk
www.LetsSign.co.uk - www.DeafBooks.co.uk

f: Let's Sign BSL
t: Let's Sign @DeafBooks

Distributedby Gardners Books
Printed in Great Britain by AlphaGraphics North East

ACKNOWLEDGEMENTS

Grateful thanks and appreciation go to;

The British Sign Language Tutor Working Group, Middlesbrough;

Susan Eastwood

Marie Greenan

Pauline Hodgson

Roy Mitchell

Sandra Teasdale

Pat Topliss

Tracy Ward

Keith Williams

Cathy Murray and colleagues, Job Centre Plus

For help with the Second Edition graphics;

The new graphics used are from
LET'S SIGN & WRITE: BSL Graphics for Sign Bilingual Materials
originally converted from bitmap to vector format with help from
Cate Detheridge of Widgit Software.

Suggestions for and help with Second Edition contents;

Mark Keane of Keane Training

*Preparing the book for publication,
innovating new working methods, and printing;*

Stephen Smith, Durham.

PREFACE TO SECOND EDITION

Since this book was first published in 2003, all of the graphics have been converted from their original bitmap, to vector format, for **LET'S SIGN & WRITE BSL Graphics for Sign Bilingual Materials** published by Widgit Software.

The graphics in this second edition and in the entire LET'S SIGN Series are included in the pack in line and colour versions, and are available for making tailor-made materials for use by trainers, tutors, teachers, families and services - in fact all those who use British Sign Language or who have contact with sign language users.

The development work on the graphics is ongoing, and users of the pack are invited to send suggestions for new graphics, with full descriptions of the signs needed, based on the handshapes and movement system used in this book to -

info@deafbooks.co.uk   Tel: 01642 580505

CONTENTS

Acknowledgements 5

Preface to the Second Edition 6

Introduction 8

Communicating in the Workplace 13

Guide to Headings and Captions 17

Direction, Orientation and Movement 18

Basic Handshapes 19

The Drawings: The Face 20

Non-Manual Features: The Face 21

About Fingerspelling 22

Fingerspelling Alphabet 24

Fingerspelling: Days of the Week 26

NUMBERS: Quick Reference Guide 28

SIGN VOCABULARY 30

Recommended Resources and Reading 110

Useful Contacts 111

INDEX..114

The Let's Sign Series...123

INTRODUCTION

Communication is a crucial factor for employment and other agencies with responsibility for providing essential services to the public. Since 1999 service providers have been required by the Disability Discrimination Act to take positive steps to make their services accessible to disabled people.

For *Deaf people whose first language is British Sign Language (BSL) and not English, improving access to information, interpreting services and communication with agency staff can be such a step.

This publication offers guidelines to those whose work will involve some degree of contact with Deaf people, since deafness is not only invisible, but its profound effects on the individual require some time, effort and imagination to fully appreciate - not an easy task in the busy lives of service providers with wide ranging responsibilities.

Many public services workers are attending BSL courses, and this is essential for learning the visual spatial structures of the language. However, it can be difficult to maintain skills when contact with sign language users is infrequent. This book can only

* The convention of the upper case 'D' in *Deaf* refers to people who identify themselves as culturally Deaf sign language users.

provide basic guidelines, but it is hoped that it can be used to support awareness and communication training, and be used as a ready reference should the need arise.

It includes information on how to optimise conditions generally for clear communication, and contains a selection of illustrated signs that should be helpful in many situations where staff come into contact with sign language users, and need to make arrangements to set up interviews involving sign language interpreters, or other communicators. It is designed to supplement interpreting services, not replace them.

The term 'deafness' covers a wide range of hearing loss and communication needs, varying from those who become deaf in later life and people who are born and grow up with deafness.

There are an estimated 8.7 million people with a degree of hearing loss that affects everyday life and communication. The huge majority will have developed or acquired hearing loss during their lives after childhood and spoken language development. They have developed as 'hearing' people and spoken language will continue to be their first language even though they may no longer be able to hear it.

Within this figure are about 60,000 who are deaf from birth or early childhood for whom English (or other spoken language) is not their first natural language in either its written or spoken form, and whose dominant language is British Sign Language.

Although much of the information in this book will have relevance to both groups, the born deaf sign language using Deaf community is its main focus.

BSL is the language of Britain's Deaf community, and in spite of regional variation (similar to dialect and accent in spoken language) it is used and understood by Deaf people throughout England, Wales, Scotland and Northern Ireland. It is subject to regional variations similar to dialect and accent in spoken language. The signs chosen here are those with wide common usage, plus examples of variations when relevant and where space allows.

The most defining feature of Deaf community membership is the experience of childhood deafness and its profound effects on language and communication. Deaf education remains a minefield of controversial issues concerning communication and language teaching methodologies in which the individual's needs may or may not be met. The consequences for many can be seriously restricted access to learning and information (and therefore general knowledge) throughout life - factors which need special consideration in all communications with deaf people.

In spite of such restrictions however, Deaf people rely mostly on lip-reading and writing for their day to day exchanges with the hearing world and interact with competence and confidence based on a lifetime's experience.

Clearly, there are more serious situations that require the services of sign language interpreters or other communicators of the Deaf person's choice. Some young Deaf people may attend with a family member, or social worker to help with communication, and personal preference should always be considered.

Others may request a sign language interpreter for interviews and consultations, and it is useful to have some understanding of the interpreter's role and code of practice.

All interpreters are bound by a strict Code of Practice and everything that is said in an assignment is strictly confidential. They are completely impartial and will not be able to give advice or views whilst working.

There is a national Register of BSL/English Interpreters and Communicators, regulated by Signature based in Durham - see page 112 in the **Useful Addresses** section at the back of this book.

The Council also publishes a Directory of Interpreters and Communicators both in print and on-line. This Directory provides details of those who are qualified and registered to provide particular interpreting or other communication services, how to contact those who are available for booking and how to use them effectively. It also provides assurance to those who use the Directory that the individuals registered have reached a level of skill necessary to offer such services for meetings/interviews, conferences and other purposes in a wide range of personal, employment, health, social care, justice and other settings.

There is a shortage of interpreters nationally and bookings need to be made well in advance, and availability cannot guaranteed.

Professional interpreters are bound by a Code of Ethics/Practice (that include the impartiality and confidentiality already referred to) and Complaints and Disciplinary Procedure.

It is suggested that your local interpreting services contact details are kept with this book.

COMMUNICATING IN THE WORKPLACE

Some general advice for clear communication for people with hearing loss

A small amount of thought and effort in communicating with deaf and hard of hearing people can make a huge difference.

For Born Deaf Sign Language Users whose main link to the world is visual, it is helpful to use

- Some basic signs and fingerspelling to support spoken communication.
- For more serious matters, an interpreter or communicator may be needed.
- Clear communication as detailed below.

For the millions of people who have become deaf as adults, or are hard of hearing, there are many practical ways of improving communication through speech and lip-reading.

Speak a little slower but keep your natural pace and rhythm - don't distort - don't shout.
Keep the message straightforward and clear.
Have pen and paper ready if needed.

Eye contact is essential

- Try to avoid moving around as you speak.
- Don't cover your mouth or talk with your head down as you write.
- Hold things up for viewing or point to them when necessary.
- Give people time to look at what you are pointing at, then back at you.
- Background noise and group discussions can make lip-reading very difficult.

Good lighting is important

- The light should be on the speaker's face.
- Try to avoid the light behind you and your face in shadow.

Facial expressions, gestures and so on make up a massive percentage of what we communicate.

- Lip-reading involves the whole face, and your expressions will convey a lot of information too.
- Some words are easier to lip-read than others.
- If there are difficulties, try saying it another way.

Approximately 5% of Deaf people have **Usher Syndrome,** a condition which combines congenital deafness with degenerative eye disease Retinitis Pigmentosa (RP), and extra consideration may need to be given to lighting and other visual conditions.

Common ways of attracting attention in the Deaf community are

- Tap an individual on the arm or shoulder.
- Make small waving movements in their line
of vision.
- Flash the lights on and off several times.

Waiting systems that rely on people responding to their name being called can cause unnecessary stress and anxiety for deaf and hard of hearing people. Systems that display numbers, or other visual means are far more suitable and effective.

There are also a number of British Sign Language information films available on video tape and DVD. The organisations in the Useful Address section at the back of this booklet can give further information and details.

GUIDE TO HEADINGS AND CAPTIONS

Languages have very few direct word for word equivalents between each other, and the headings given for each sign are a guide to meaning rather than a direct translation.

The captions are intended to give extra information on the handshape, location and movement of signs.

Details of non-manual features (***facial/bodily expressions***) ***variation,*** and changes in ***context*** are given in ***bold italics*** when relevant and where space allows. Additional meanings are given in **BOLD CAPITALS**.

Signs and fingerspelling are described and illustrated as if the signer is right-handed, with the right hand always referred to as R. and the left hand as L.

Left-handed signers will use the reverse of this, with the left hand as dominant.

From the thumb, the fingers are referred to as index, middle, ring and little finger.

ORIENTATION, DIRECTION AND MOVEMENT

The direction the hands may face, point or move are described as if the hands are open.

As illustrated below the R. hand is palm left and the L. hand is palm right. They can also be described as palm facing, or palm in.

The hands may be described as '*pointing*' up, forward etc even if the fingers are bent in a different direction or closed.

As illustrated both hands are pointing forward, palms facing.

If the handshapes are described, for example, as *index and thumb extended*, then it is understood that the other fingers are closed.

Diagonal movements are described '*forward/left*' or '*back/right*' and so on.

BASIC HANDSHAPES

Closed Hand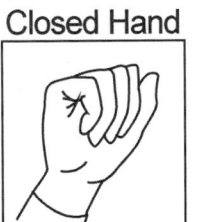
Flat Hand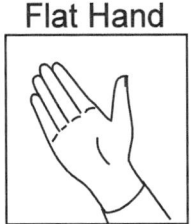
Clawed Hand
Fist

Bent Hand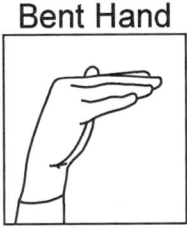
Open Hand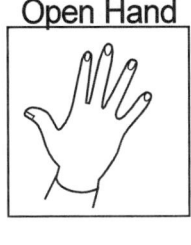
Bunched Hand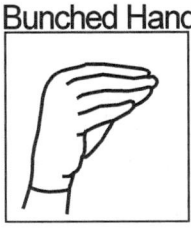
'L' Hand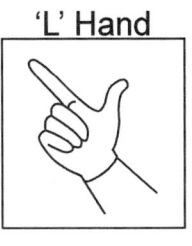

'M' Hand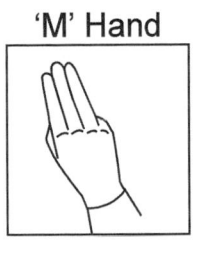
'N' Hand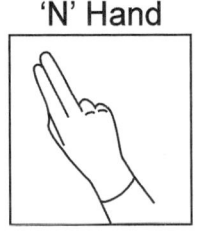
'V' Hand
'Y' Hand

'O' Hand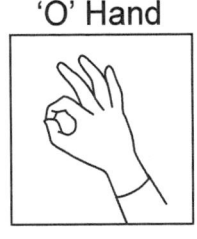
Full 'O' Hand
'C' Hand
Full 'C' Hand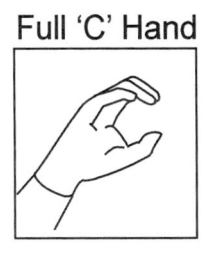

Irish 'T Hand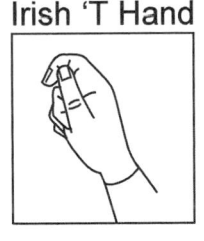

Frequently used handshapes in BSL and terms used in this book to describe them.

The fingers are identified (from the thumb) as *index, middle finger, ring finger* and *little finger.*

THE DRAWINGS: The Face

The drawings show the important components of the signs as clearly as possible without distracting background details. One of the most important of these components is the face.

Learners typically focus on the hands and movement of the signs and tend to neglect the importance of the face, at least in the early stages. Communication in BSL however starts with eye contact, and the face is the focal point throughout.

Signing can be dull or even meaningless without good and appropriate facial clues or if part of the face is obscured by dark glasses, beard, or moustache for example.

The facial expressions in the drawings are appropriate to some signs in some contexts, but not all the possibilities can be shown. BSL uses a range of eye, mouth and facial movements that have grammatical functions in that they can add to, modify or change meaning.

These are termed **non-manual features** (as in the sign at the top left of the next page) and they are referred to and described in the captions where space permits.

Some excellent photographic examples and details of BSL grammar can be found in the books detailed in Recommended Resources and Reading.

NON-MANUAL FEATURES: The Face

ABOUT FINGERSPELLING

Fingerspelling is a manual representation of the letters of the alphabet. Drawings give a static image of the alphabet, but in fluent use, the shapes can merge and appear quite different. They are recognised as word patterns, and this requires practice.

- Fingerspelling is an important and integral part of BSL but relies on the understanding of English and should be used with caution.

- Its use varies considerably between individuals.

- It is rarely used to spell out whole phrases or sentences.

- It is commonly used for names and places.

- It is used for acronyms eg **BSL**, **GCSE, NVQ, ATW (Access to Work)** - see examples **HGV, CV, DEA, DLA** opposite.

- Words can be spelt out in full, abbreviated or initialised - see examples **TV** and **TT** *(toilet)* opposite.

- Days of the week and months of the year can also be signed with a repeated initial or abbreviated pattern, e.g. **Wednesday** - **WW**, *January* - **JAN**, and so on.

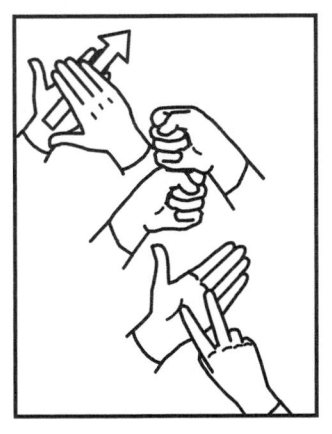
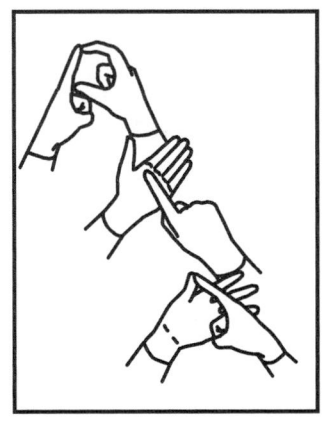
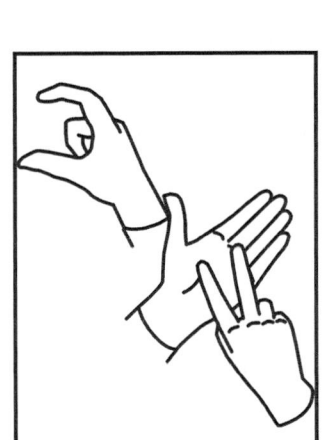
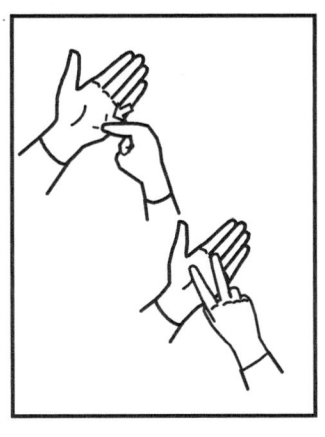
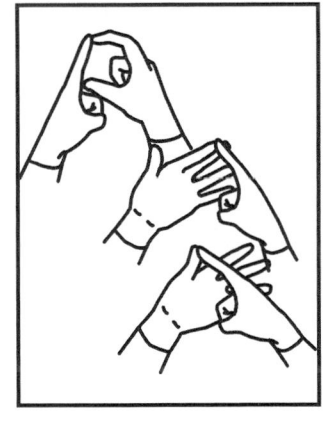
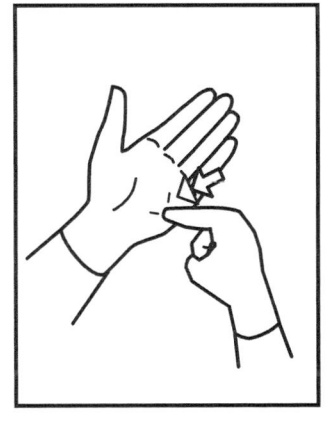

BRITISH FINGERSPELLING ALPHABET
LEFT-HANDED VERSION

BRITISH FINGERSPELLING ALPHABET
RIGHT-HANDED VERSION

FINGERSPELLING: Days of the Week

Days of the week are commonly based on fingerspelling. These are usually abbreviated forms as shown in the illustrations opposite.

In addition to the example of MONDAY represented by 'MON', a repeated 'MM' is also alternatively used. TUESDAY may be represented by 'TU' 'TT', or 'TUES', WEDNESDAY by 'WED' or 'WW', THURSDAY by 'TH', and FRIDAY by 'FRI' or 'FF', and other similar variations.

SUNDAY can be signed as in the last illustration with the flat hands tapping together twice, although SATURDAY and SUNDAY do have alternative signs in some regions.

Months of the year are similarly fingerspelt abbreviations or the shorter words are spelt in full, eg MAY, JUNE.

A separate 'days of the week' system is mainly used in Scotland. The index finger and thumb close together twice for MONDAY, the middle finger and thumb for TUESDAY, the ring finger and thumb for WEDNESDAY and little finger and thumb for THURSDAY.

FRIDAY is signed with R. palm left 'V' hand moving right to left across the chin. SATURDAY is a repeated downward opening movement of a closed hand held under the chin, and SUNDAY is palm left R. flat hand bending back to contact upper chest twice. SATURDAY and SUNDAY also have alternative versions in some regions.

DAYS OF THE WEEK

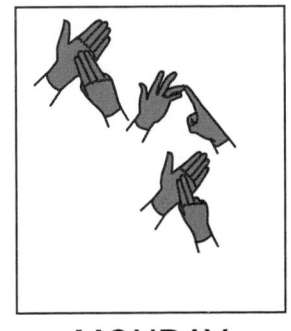
MONDAY

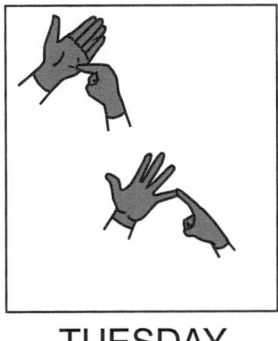
TUESDAY

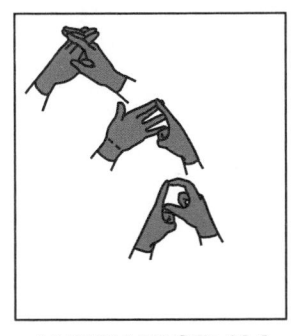
WEDNESDAY

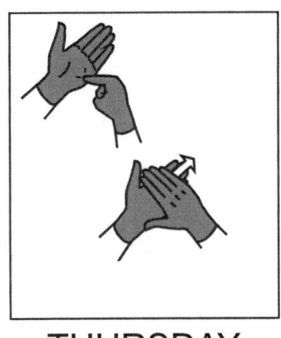
THURSDAY

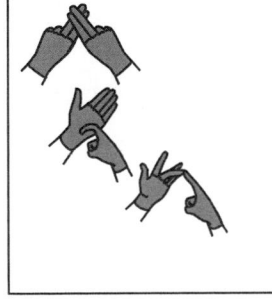
FRIDAY

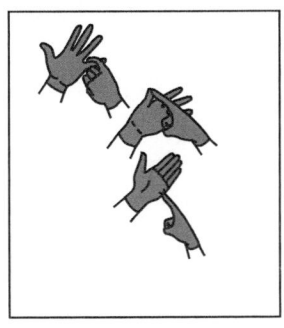
SATURDAY

There are other variations for signing days of the week, but these are commonly used and understood examples used in BSL.

SUNDAY

NUMBERS: Quick Reference Guide

Numbers are notorious for their regional variations. It is not possible to show them all in this simple guide, but the two most commonly used and understood systems are illustrated. Learners need to be aware of their own regional versions and variations used in other areas.

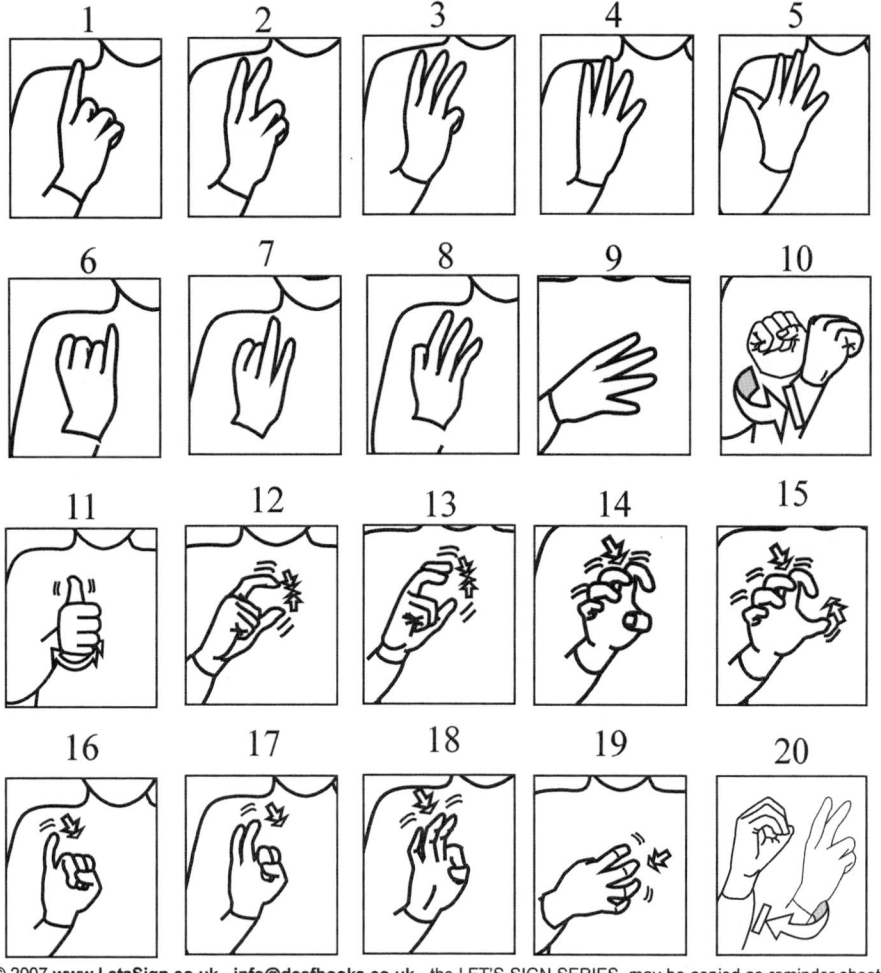

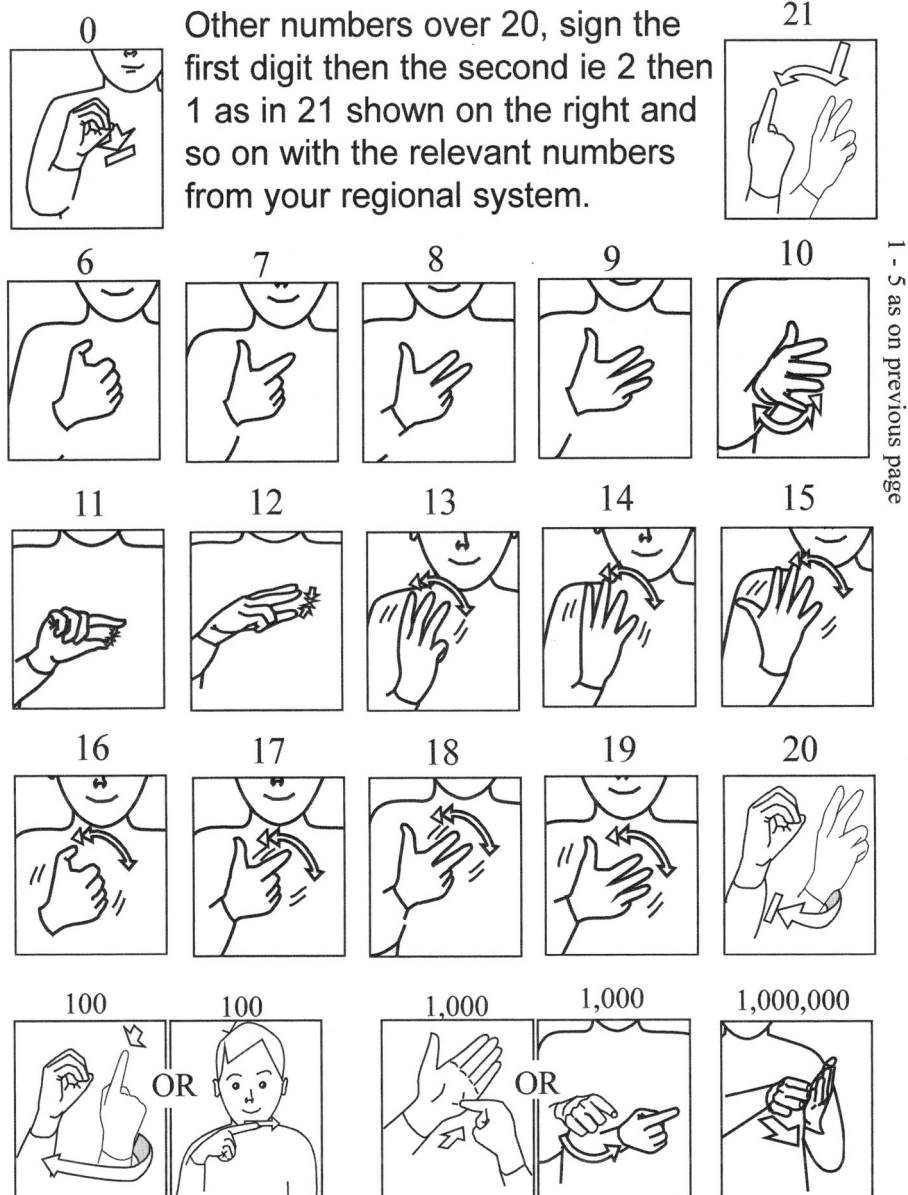

SIGN VOCABULARY

ACCESS, GO THROUGH

R. flat hand moves forward/left between fingers of L. hand. With sharp movement, also means **BUTT IN, INTERRUPT**. *Directional.*

ADDRESS, LIVE

Tip of middle finger (or clawed hand) rubs up and down on side of chest. Also *regional* sign for **TOILET**.

ADVICE, ADVISE/R

R. index moves from mouth then changes to a closed hand with thumb up on L. palm and hands move forward together.

AFTER, AFTERWARDS

Palm down R. closed hand with thumb out moves over L. in small arc. Flat hand can be used. Also means **THEN**. *Varies*.

AFTER, LATER

Palm forward index finger moves sideways in small arc. Movement may repeat. *Varies*.

AFTERNOON

Tips of 'N' hand touch chin, then hand twists from wrist to point forwards.

AGAIN, REPEAT

Palm left 'V' hand makes short quick shaking movements forward/down from the wrist. Also means **FREQUENTLY, OFTEN.**

AGREE, AGREEMENT

Closed hands with thumbs up contact knuckles together. The head nods, lips pressed together. Also means **APPROPRIATE, SUIT/ABLE.**

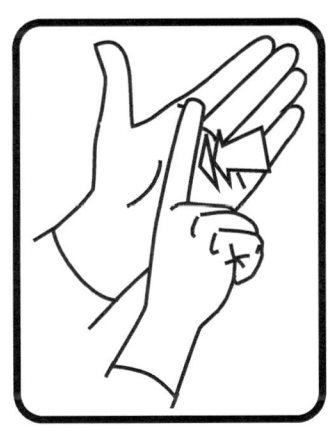

ALARM, BELL (clock, fire)

Side of extended R. index finger bangs twice against the L. palm. Index waggles forward/down for **CLOCK.** See also **FIRE.**

ALRIGHT, FINE, OK
Closed hands with thumbs up and pointing slightly out move in outward circles. Eyebrows raised for *'are you ok?'* etc.

APPOINT, EMPLOY
Full 'C' hand moves inwards from the side. Also means **SUBSTITUTE, SUPPLY**.

AREA, LOCAL, PLACE
Palm down open hand makes horizontal circular movements. Also means **REGION**.

ARRIVE, REACH, GET TO
R. bent hand moves in forward arc to contact L. palm held forward.

ASK, APPLY, REMIND
Palm forward bent hand makes two short forward movements (*directional*). Also means **PESTER** (firm movements).

ASK, REQUEST
R. 'O' hand near side of mouth, moves forward in small arc. *Directional.*

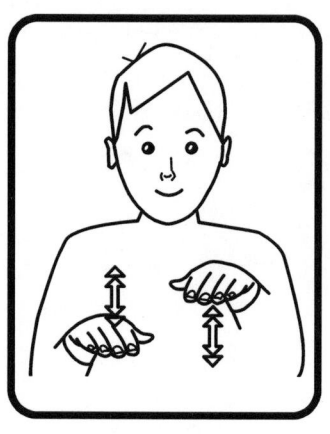

ASSESS/MENT
Hands move alternately up and down several times, palm up or palm down. 'N' hands can also be used.

BAD, WRONG
Extended little finger makes short movement forward. May repeat.

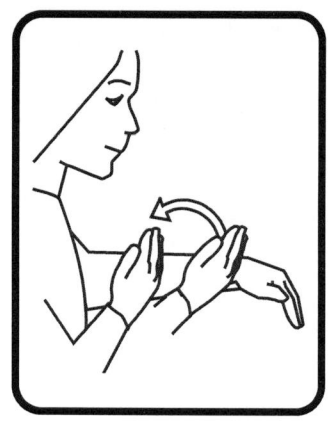

BEFORE, EARLIER, EARLY
R. flat hand moves from wrist up left forearm in small arc. *Varies.*

BEFORE, PAST, PREVIOUS

R. flat hand moves backwards over right shoulder several times. Refers to **IN THE PAST**, as in *'I worked there before'*.

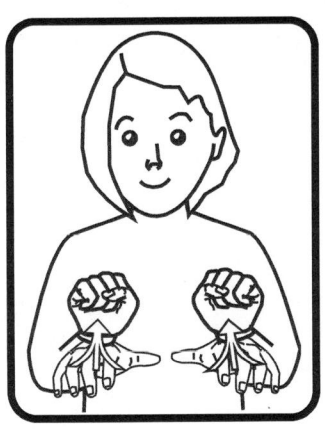

BEGIN, START

Open hands palm down/back snap closed as hands twist to palm forward. ***Varies.***

BEST

Tip of R. extended thumb brushes forward sharply against top of L. extended thumb.

BISCUIT
Tips of R. clawed hand tap twice against left elbow. May *vary.*

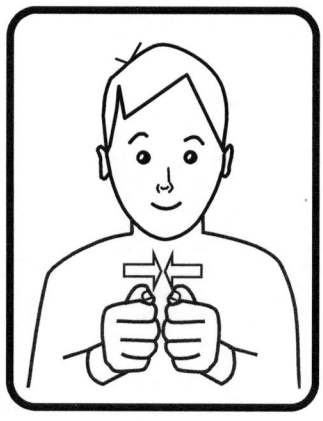

BOOK (to), APPOINTMENT
Closed hands come together to contact at the knuckles.

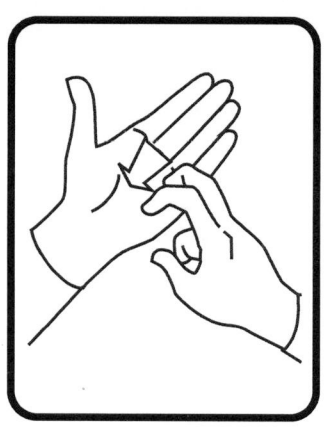

BOOK (to), CONTRACT
Tips of bent R. 'V' hand contact L. palm. Also means **RESERVE** or **MAKE A BOOKING** eg of an interpreter.

BORE/D, BORING, YAWN

Flat hand taps chin several times with mouth slightly open as if stifling a yawn.

BOSS/Y, MANAGER, HEAD

Index fingers pointing forward/up twist sharply up/back from wrist. May be one hand only. Also means **AUTHORITY, EMPLOYER, CHIEF**.

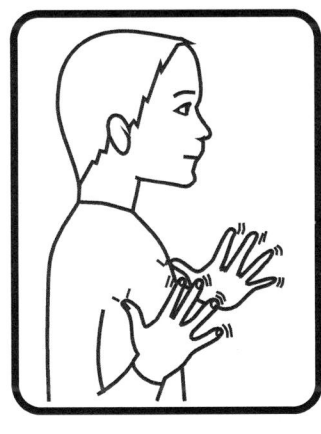

BREAK, LEISURE, REST

Thumb tips of open hands (or one hand) on chest, fingers may wiggle. Head may tilt. Also means **RELAX**.

BRING, FETCH
Irish 'T' hands move simultaneously from right to left in small arc, or in *direction* to suit context.

BUS, LORRY, TRUCK, VAN
Palm up closed hands make wide flat steering movements. Also means **DRIVE, DRIVER.**

BUS, TUBE, UNDERGROUND
Fingers of bent 'V' hand make short movement forward (or down) at shoulder height (*regional*).

BUSINESS
Little finger edge of palm up flat hand taps into side of body twice.

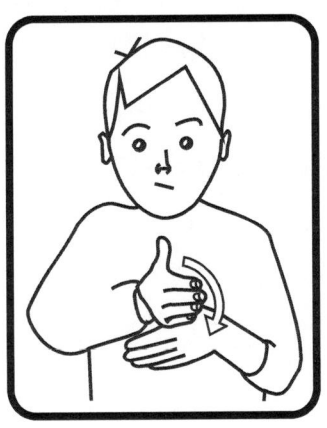

BUSY, HARD WORK
R. flat hand swivels forward/down over back of L. Cheeks may be puffed.

BYE, GOODBYE, CHEERIO
Hand moves side to side in waving movement, or flat hand bends repeatedly from palm knuckle.

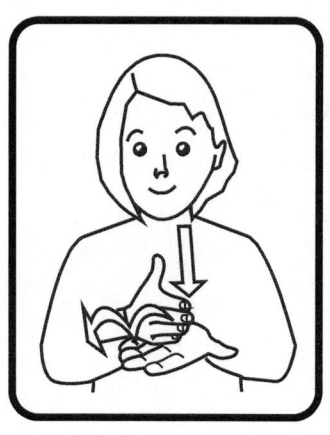

CAR PARK
Edge of R. flat hand (vehicle classifier) contacts L. palm several times with small movements to the right, like cars in a row.

CAR, DRIVE, DRIVER
Closed hands move in action of holding and moving a steering wheel. **DRIVE** may be short forward movement of both hands.

CERTIFICATE
'O' hands held apart, one higher than the other, make small repeated shaking movements. Also means **QUALIFICATION.**

CHANGE, ALTER, CONVERT

Irish 'T' hands (or upright index fingers) held palms facing twist round each other to finish crossed over. **Varies.**

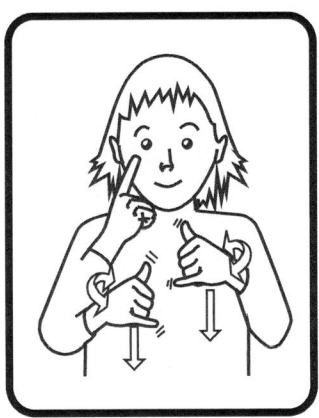

CHECK, TEST, TRY OUT

Index moves down from eye, then 'Y' hands (or just one hand) move down in waggling movements from wrists. **Directional.**

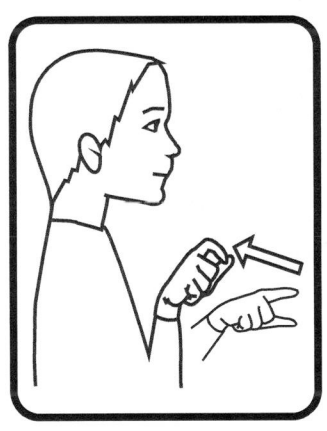

CHOOSE, PICK, SELECT

Index finger closes onto thumb as hand moves backwards. May repeat, and with two hands alternately. **Directional**. Also means **INVITE**.

CLAIM
Flat hand moves sharply down/forward to finish palm up.

COACH, BUS
Full 'C' hands, one in front of the other, pull diagonally apart, forward/back.

COFFEE
'C' hand makes short quick twisting movements near side of mouth or R. fist grinds on top of L. *Varies.*

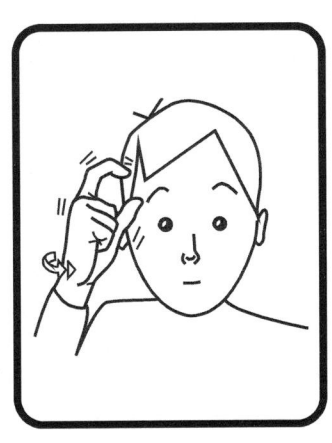

COLLEGE
'C' hand makes short quick twisting movements from the wrist near the side of forehead. **Varies.**

COMMUNICATE
Full 'C' hands (or 'C' hands) move backwards and forwards alternately. Also means **COMMUNICATION, COMMUNICATOR.**

COMPUTER, KEYBOARD
Fingers of palm down hands wiggle. Also means **TYPE**. May be combined sign for **SCREEN**.

CONFIDENTIAL
Clawed hands move inwards, one in front of the other in front of the mouth closing sharply to fists.

CONTACT, LINK, JOIN
Hands move towards each other and fingers of 'O' hands interlock.
Directional. Also means **CONNECT, CONNECTION.**

CONTINUE, CARRY ON
Palm down 'C' hands (or just one hand) move simultaneously to the right, or forwards. Also means **PERMANENT.**

CORRIDOR, HALL
'N' hands move forward at sides of head. Flat hands can be used. Also means **PASSAGE**.

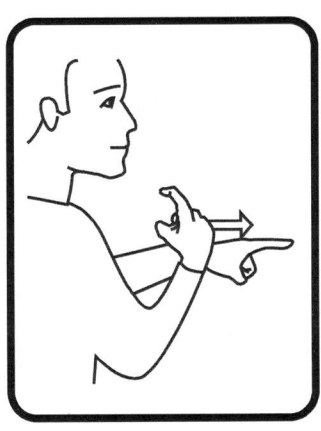

COURSE, SCHEME
Edge of R 'C' hand moves forward along L. hand.

COURT, TRIAL, TRIBUNAL
'N' hands move alternately up and down. Can be palm up or palm down or use flat hands. Also means **ASSESS/MENT**.

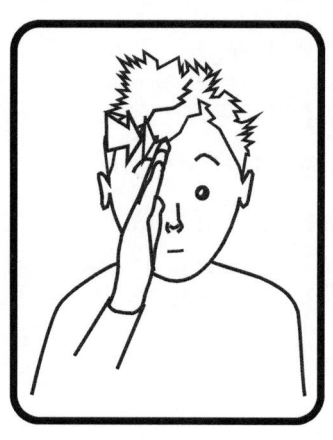

DANGER, DANGEROUS

Edge of R. flat hand comes up sharply to forehead. May tap twice on forehead.

DAY, DAWN, LIGHT

Palm back open hands start crossed and swing upwards and apart. **DAY** is often also fingerspelt.

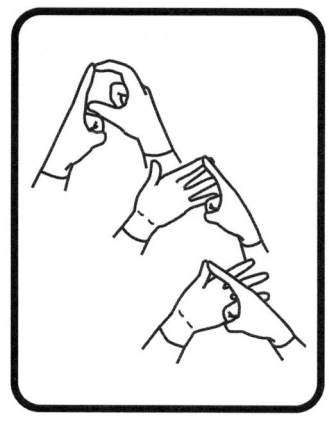

DEA
DISABILITY EMPLOYMENT ADVISER

Sign the three signs, or fingerspell 'DEA'.

DEAF, DEAF PERSON
'N' hand contacts ear. Cheeks may be puffed for **PROFOUNDLY DEAF, REALLY DEAF.**

DIFFERENT, DIFFERENCE
Index fingers held together twist over and apart.

DIRECT, STRAIGHT
Flat hand bends forward from the wrist as it moves forward from in front of nose. Also means **STRAIGHT ON.**

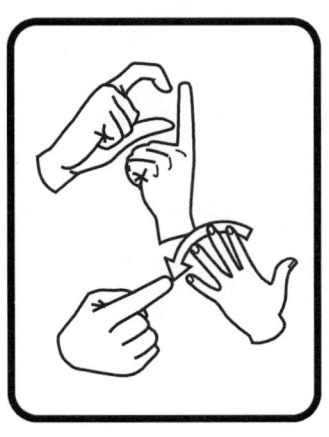

DISABILITY, DISABLED
Hands form fingerspelt 'D' then R. index brushes down along the tips of L. fingers.

DISAGREE, DON'T AGREE
Closed hands with thumbs up touch at knuckles, then spring open and apart as the head shakes.

DISAPPOINT/MENT
Tips of 'V' hand prod neck, may repeat. Lips pressed together and turned down. Also **FRUSTRATED, MISS** (*regional*).

DOCTOR, MEDICAL
Tips of 'O' hand contact right, then left sides of chest. **Varies.**

DON'T KNOW
Flat hand swings down to palm up from forehead as shoulders shrug, head shakes, lips pressed together.

DON'T LIKE, DISLIKE
Open hand on chest twists forwards/up as head shakes with negative expression. May move palm down away from body.

DON'T WANT, DON'T NEED
Flat hand moves firmly down and away from body as head shakes.

E-MAIL
Index fingers flick off thumbs towards each other. Can be one hand only. ***Directional.***

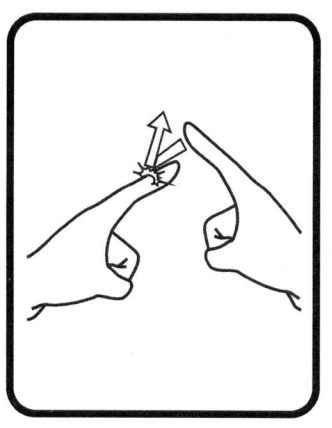

EARLY, EMERGENCY
R. index bangs sharply on L. index and bounces up again. Also means **QUICK, SUDDEN, URGENT**.

EASY, SIMPLE, SOFT
Index finger prods into the cheek twice. The cheeks may be puffed.

EAT, FOOD
Bunched hand makes two short movements to the mouth. Also means **LUNCH, SUPPER.**

EMPLOYER, MANAGER
Thumbs of 'Y' hands jab into sides of upper chest. Also means **BOSS, CHIEF, OWNER** etc. One of several variations.

EVENING, NIGHT
Palm back flat hands swing in/down to finish crossed. **Varies.**

EXPERIENCE
Thumb tip touches forehead then moves down changing to flat hand with fingertips brushing down past L. palm. Also means **KNOW ABOUT**. **Varies.**

EXPLAIN, TELL ABOUT
Flat hands rotate round each other in forward circles eg '*I'll explain*' or backwards eg '*explain to me*'. **Directional.**

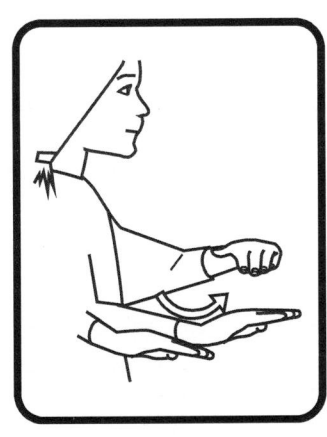

FAX, SEND A FAX

R. flat hand moves down/forward in small arc under L. or twists round and moves back to signer *(directional).*

FED UP, SICK OF, ENOUGH

Bent hand bangs up against underside of chin. May repeat. Shoulders and corners of mouth droop.

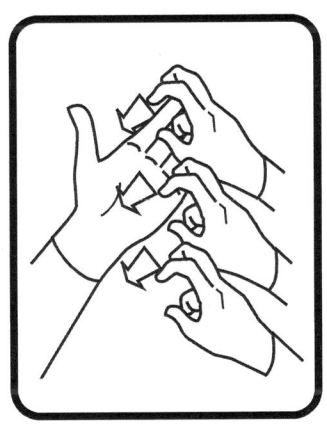

FILL IN FORM, NOTES

Tips of bent 'V' hand (or 'N' hand) make short movements towards L. palm several times, moving down.

FINGERSPELL, SPELL
Fingers and thumbs wiggle against each other as hands move to the right. Refers to two handed fingerspelling.

FINISH, END, STOP
Fingers of bent hands close onto thumbs in short firm downward movement.

FINISH/ED, COMPLETED
Closed hands with thumbs up and pointing slightly out move in outward circles. *Regional.*

FIRE ESCAPE
Palm facing hands move up, fingers wiggling **(FIRE)**, then R. extended index moves sharply forward under palm down L. hand.

FIRE, BURN, FLAMES
Fingers of palm facing open hands wiggle as hands move up and down alternately. May *vary in context.*

GIVE, OFFER, LET
Palm up hands (or just one) move in forward arc or in *direction* to suit context. Also means **GIFT, PRESENT.**

GO, GONE, WENT, SENT
Index finger swings forward/up from wrist to point forward. *Varies.*

GOING TO, INTEND
Back of extended thumb taps side of upper chest twice. Lips are stretched. Also means **ANTICIPATE, EXPECT.**

GOOD, GREAT, HELLO
Closed hand (or both hands) with thumb up makes short movement forward.

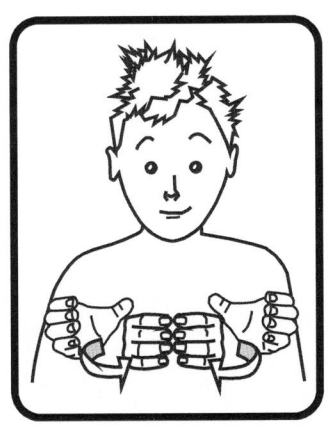

GROUP, TEAM

Full 'C' hands move in twisting at the wrists to touch together at fingertips. **Varies**.

HAPPEN, ARISE, CROP UP

R. index moves sharply up behind L. hand, or makes upward flicking movement in front of L. hand.

HAPPY, ENJOY, GLAD

Hands make repeated contact brushing against each other, with pleased expression.

HARD, DIFFICULT/Y
Tip of R. thumb prods into L. palm twice, eyebrows furrowed.

HAVE A LOOK, LET'S SEE
Tip of index finger taps cheek just below eye twice.   Also means **CHECK OUT**.

HAVE TO, COMPULSORY
Flat hands held apart make short firm downward movement with stress. Also means **MUST**.

HAVE, GET, POSSESS/ION

Palm up clawed hand makes slight downward movement as it closes firmly.

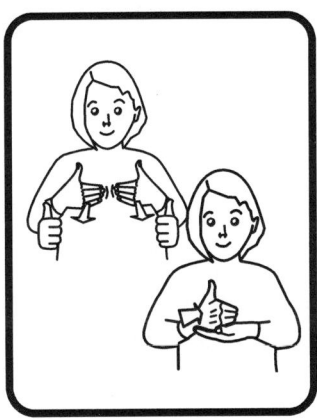

HEALTH AND SAFETY

Tips of flat hands touch chest, and move forward, thumbs up, then edge of R. bent hand on L. palm as hands move back.

HEARING (not deaf)

Index finger moves from ear to mouth. May finish with repeated tap on chin.

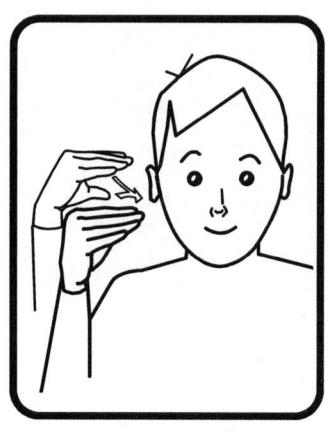

HEARING LOSS, DEAFENED
Fingers close onto thumb near ear with downward movement. Also means **LOSE HEARING, BECOME DEAF.** Or fingerspell 'HOH' for **HARD OF HEARING.**

HELLO
Closed hands with thumbs up twist sharply over from palm down to palms facing.

HELLO, HI
Flat hand with thumb tucked in makes short movement out from near side of head. *Varies*.

HELP/ER, ASSISTANT
Closed hand with thumb up rests on L. palm as both hands move forward. ***Directional.*** Also means **SUPPORT**.

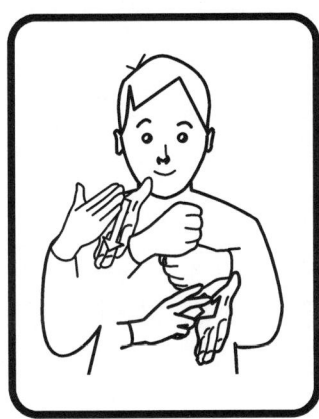

HGV
Fingerspell 'HGV'.

HOLIDAY
Flat hands move from sides of head, twisting to palm forward, slightly down and apart. ***Varies.***

HOLIDAY, CELEBRATION
Irish 'T' hands make circling movements near sides of head, or same movement with extended middle fingers *(regional)*.

HOME
Tips of flat hands touch, with hands held at an angle.

HOPE, HOPEFULLY, WISH
Fingers are held crossed, palm forward. May be one hand only. ***Varies***.

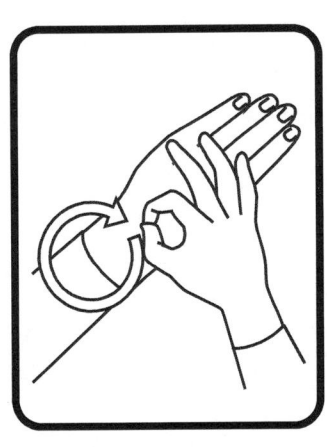

HOUR
R. 'O' hand moves round in circle over left wrist or palm, or R. extended index twists round in full circle. **Varies**.

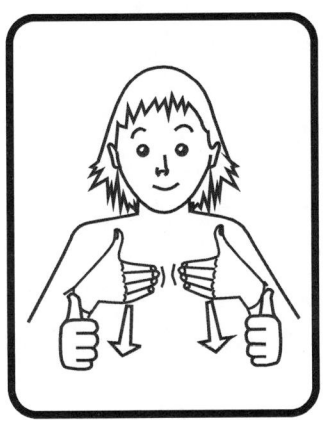

HOW ARE YOU?
Tips of bent hands on chest; hands move forward closing with thumbs up, eyebrows raised. Also means **ARE YOU WELL?**

HOW OLD? WHAT AGE?
Fingers wiggle in front of nose. Eyebrows are raised or furrowed.

ILL, ILLNESS, NOT WELL
Little fingers (or just one) brush down chest, head may tilt, may repeat. Also a *regional* sign for **TIRED**.

IMPORTANT, CRUCIAL
R. open hand comes down to land on tip of L. index. May tap twice. Also means **TOP**.

IMPROVE, IMPROVEMENT
Tips of R. 'O' hand move upwards on upright L. index finger. Also means **GET BETTER**.

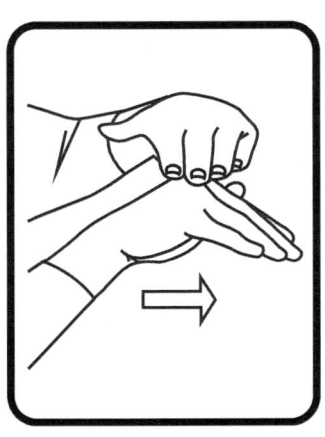

IN, GO IN, ENTER, ENTRY

R. bent hand straightens to a flat hand as it moves forward under L. hand.

INCOME, EARNINGS

Palm up clawed hand moves in/down to body twice, closing to a fist. Also means **BENEFIT, DOLE, PENSION, WAGES** and other forms of income.

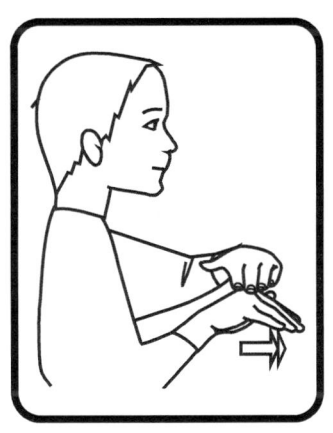

INDOORS, INSIDE

R. bent hand makes two short movements under L. hand.

INFORM, INFORMATION

Palm back extended index fingers move quickly forwards and backwards from the mouth.

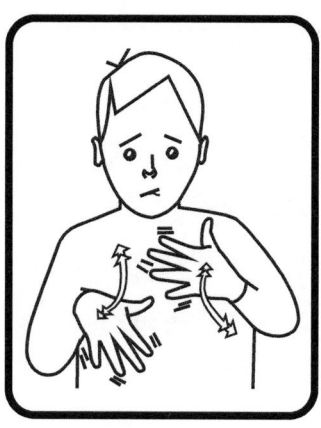

INJURY, HURT

Palm back open hands shake up and down from the wrists alternately in front of the body with pained expression.

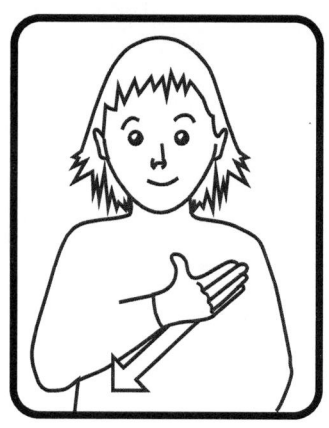

INSURE, INSURANCE

Edge of R. bent hand moves diagonally down across the chest.

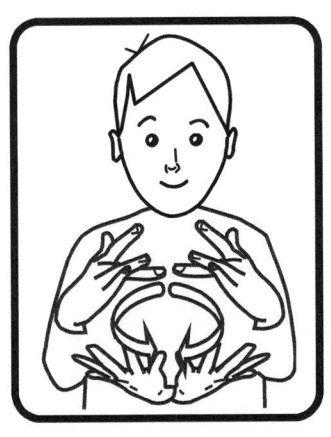

INTERNET, NET, WEB
Tips of middle fingers touch briefly, then hands move out and round in sphere shape.

INTERPRET/ER
'V' hands (or 'N' hands) twist alternately backwards and forwards from the wrists.

INTERVIEW, CONVERSE
Palm facing index fingers move forward and back to the mouth alternately.
Also means **DIALOGUE, DISCUSS.**

INTERVIEW, ENQUIRY

Tips of R. 'O' hand makes repeated contact with L. index in circular movements.

JOIN, ATTACH, LINK

Hands move towards each other and fingers of 'O' hands interlock.

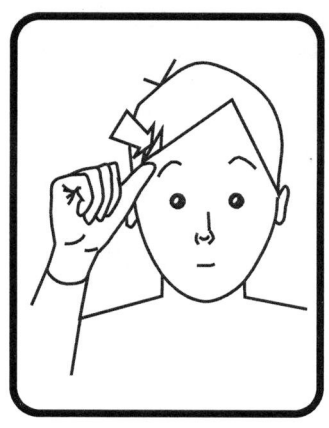

KNOW

Thumb tip taps on side of forehead.

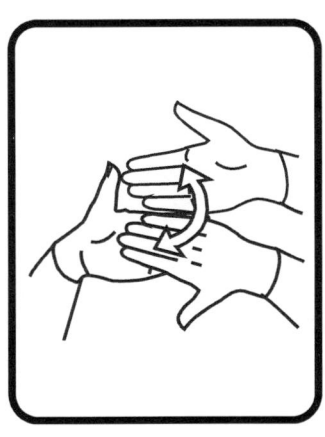

LAPTOP COMPUTER
Palm back flat hands, R. on top of L. twists over to contact L. palm, then back again.

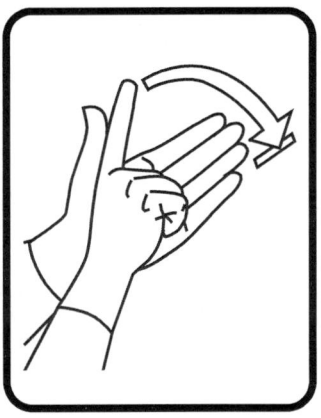

LATE, OVERDUE
R. extended index twists sharply forward/down across L. palm.

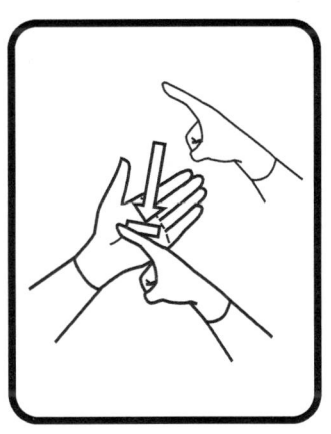

LAW, RULE, PRINCIPLE
Edge of R. index finger lands sharply on L. palm.

LAZY, IDLE
R. bent hand taps left elbow twice, tip of tongue between teeth. Also one version of **BISCUIT**.

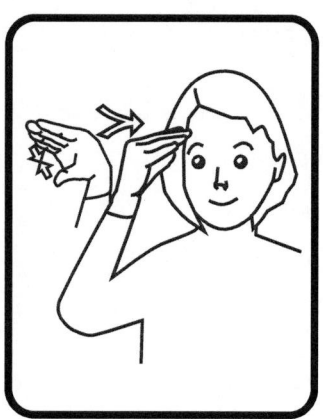

LEARN, ACQUIRE, TAKE IN
Palm forward hand (or both hands) twists back to side of head, closing to a bunched hand. *Varies*.

LEAVE, GO, DEPART
Palm back flat hand swings forward/right from wrist to finish palm down.

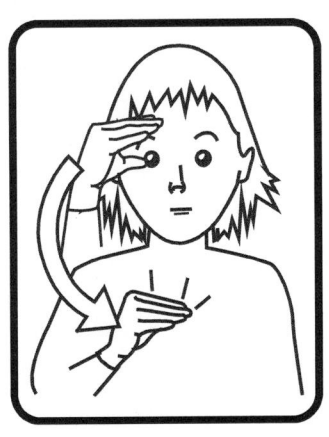

LET ME KNOW
Bent hand with thumb out moves down from forehead to contact body closing to a bunched hand.

LET YOU KNOW
Bent hand with thumb out moves down from forehead and forward or in *direction* of person referred to, closing to a bunched hand.

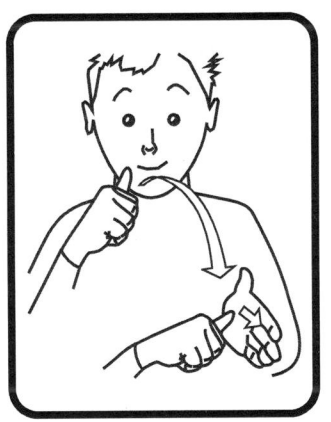

LETTER, MAIL, STAMP
Tip of extended thumb touches lips, then moves down to contact L. palm.
Also *regional* INSURANCE.

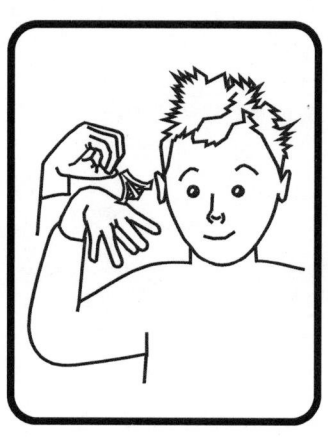

LIGHT (on), PUT LIGHT ON
Full 'O' hand springs down/open. Can be *located* to suit context, both hands for plural.

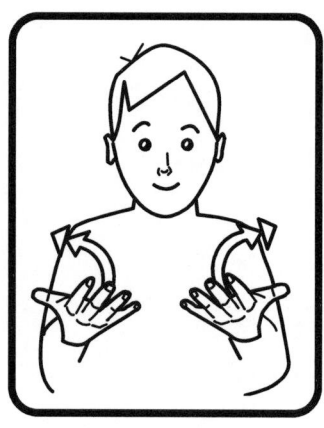

LIGHT (weight)
Palm up open hands make upward wafting movements.

LOOK AFTER, SUPERVISE
R. 'V' hand on top of L. at an angle; hands move down from near eye.

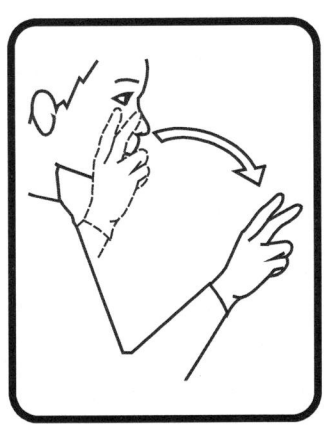

LOOK, LOOK AT, SEE

'V' hand (eye gaze classifier) makes short movement forward, or in *direction* to suit context.

LUCK/Y, GOOD LUCK

Thumb tip of 'L' hand brushes down from nose as hand twists to palm down. *Varies*.

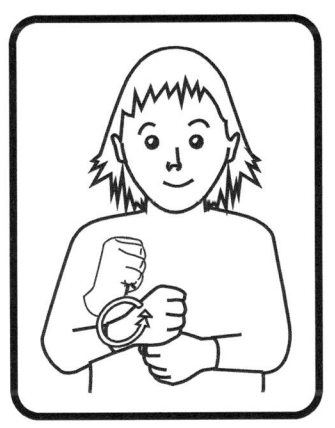

MAKE, DO, REPAIR, MEND

Edge of R. fist bangs top of L. fist in circular movements.

MAYBE, MIGHT, PERHAPS
'Y' hand waggles quickly from wrist, lips stretched.

MEET
Upright index fingers (person classifiers) held apart, move in towards each other. *Directional*.

MEETING, CONFERENCE
Index fingers circle round each other.

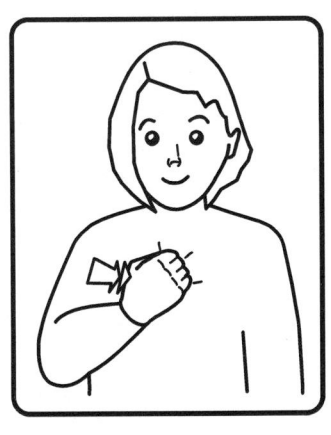

MINE, MY, MY OWN

Closed hand makes two small taps on upper chest. Can also be signed with single contact. Also means **BELONGS TO ME.**

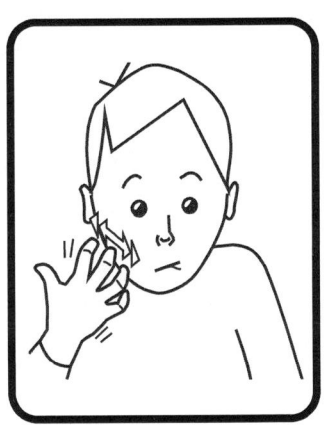

MISTAKE, ERROR, SORRY

Clawed hand makes small shaking movements near chin or side of head. *Varies*. Also means **ACCIDENT.**

MOBILE-PHONE

Hand with fingers tightly curled held at side of face.

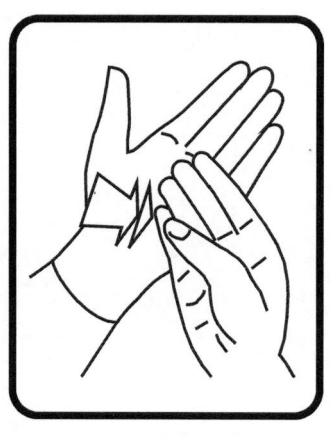

MONEY, CASH, FINANCE

Backs of fingers of R. bunched hand tap L. palm twice. **Varies**.

MORNING, GOOD MORNING

Fingertips of R. bent hand (with thumb up) touch left then right side of chest. **Varies**.

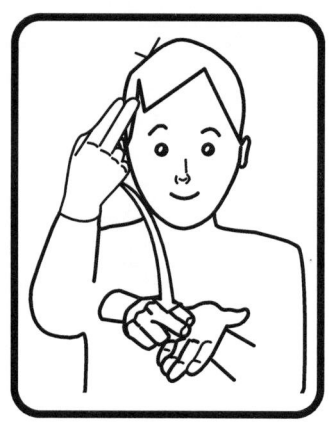

NAME DOWN, ENROL

Tips of 'N' hand on side of forehead move down to contact L. palm. Also means **SIGN FOR**.

NAME, CALLED
Tips of 'N' hand touch side of forehead, then move and twist forward.

NEGOTIATE, CONSULT
Palm up flat hands move backwards and forwards several times. Also means **DEALINGS, TRADE.**

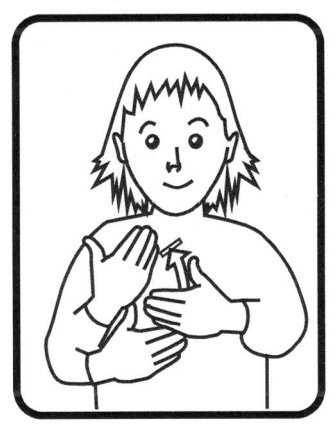

NEW, FRESH, LATEST
R. flat hand brushes sharply up behind L.

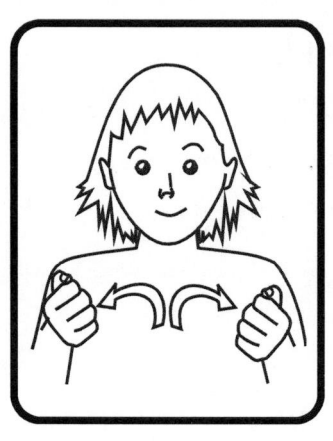

NEWSPAPER, MAGAZINE
Hands twist over and apart in action of holding and opening a newspaper. Also means **CATALOGUE.**

NEXT TO, BESIDE
Closed hands with thumbs extended; R. hand twists from the wrist to the right, away from L. hand

NEXT, AFTER, THEN, TURN
Extended thumb twists over from palm down to palm up. *Directional*.

NICE, SWEET, APPETISING

R. thumb moves across chin from left to right.

NOT YET, BEFORE, WAIT

Palm forward closed hands make short repeated movements in towards each other as head shakes with 'shh' lip-pattern.

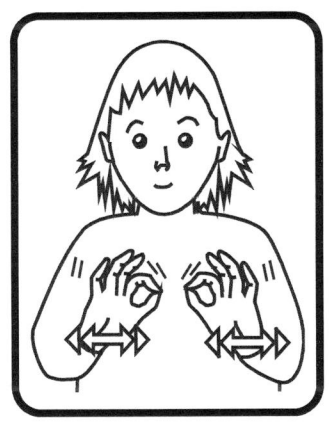

NOTHING, NONE, NOBODY

'O' hands (or full 'O' hands) shake from side to side, or make repeated circles towards each other. Tongue tip may protrude.

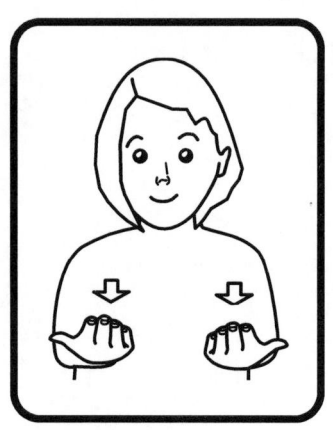

NOW
Palm up flat hands make single short movement down. Firm movement for **RIGHT NOW.**

NUMBER, DATE, MATHS
Knuckles of closed hand tap chin twice. With raised eyebrows can also mean **HOW MANY?**

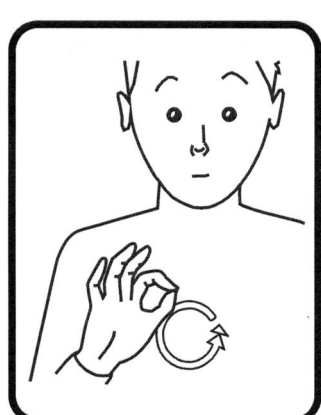

OFFICE
Palm forward 'O' hand moves round in small circles. *Varies.*

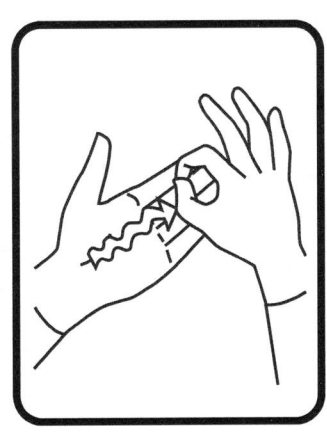

OFFICE, SECRETARY
'O' hand moves along L. palm with small squiggling movements. **Varies**.

OUTSIDE, ABROAD
Bent hand makes two short forward movements. Also means **FOREIGN/ER**.

PAPER
Tap knuckles of both closed hands together twice. One of several *variations*.

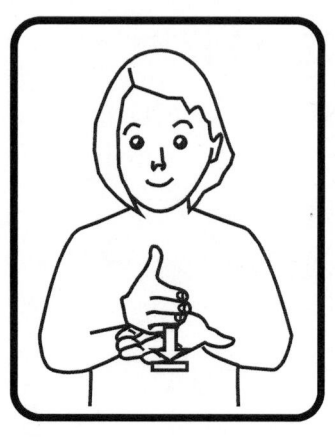

PARK, STATIONARY (car)
Edge of R. flat hand rests on L. palm; hands make short movement down.

PARTIALLY DEAF
R. flat hand is drawn down across L. palm, then 'N' hand touches ear.

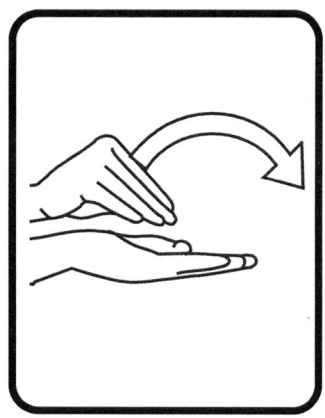

PAY, PAYMENT, PAY FOR
R. bunched hand (or Irish T hand) moves forward from L. palm in small arc. ***Directional***.

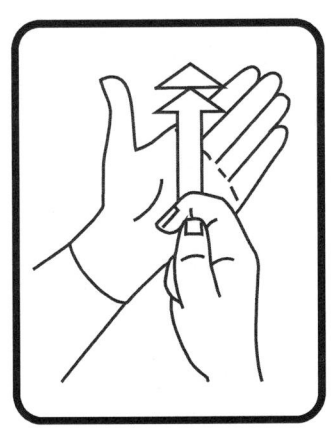

PAY, PAYMENTS, RENT

R. Irish 'T' hand moves forward from L. palm several times. Also means **MORTGAGE** and other regular payments.

PEOPLE

Palm forward index finger moves down in short zigzag or index finger, palm left with little finger up, taps chin twice. *Regional*.

PEOPLE, HUMAN, PUBLIC

Index and thumb close together as they brush down chin, then index finger brushes forward on cheek.

PERSONAL PAGER
Fingers vibrate rapidly against thumb near waist. Vibrating Pagers are used by deaf people, to alert to baby, doorbell, fire, or other alarm systems.

PLEASE, THANKS
Tips of flat hand touch mouth, then hand swings forward/down to finish palm up.

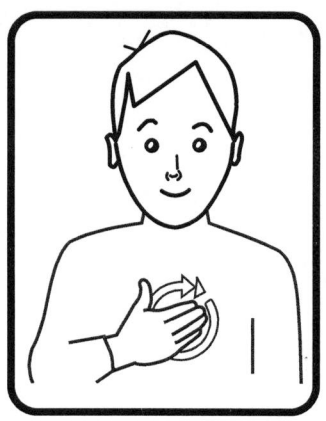

PLEASED, HAPPY, GLAD
Flat hand rubs in circles on chest with pleased expression, or flat hands brush emphatically against each other.

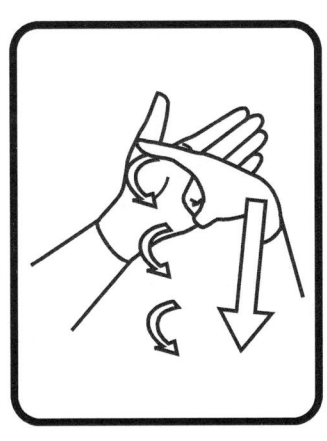

POLICY, RULES

R. index moves down/back from L. palm, or down left arm in small hops. Also means **PRINCIPLES, REGULATIONS.**

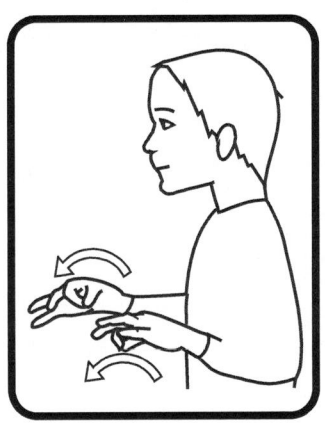

POSTPONE, DELAY

'O' hands move forward together in small arc. Also means, **PUT OFF.** The hands move back for **BRING FORWARD.**

PRIVATE, SECRET

Index edge of flat hand taps twice against the lips. *Varies.*

QUALIFICATION/S
Hands form fingerspelt 'Q' and make short movement down. Also means **QUALIFIED,** and **QUALITY.**

QUESTION, QUERY
Palm forward 'O' hand moves round in small circle, then makes short forward movement.

QUICK, FAST, HURRY
R. index taps on L. several times very quickly.

READ
R. 'V' hand (eye gaze classifier) sweeps from side to side above L. palm. **Direction** and movement will suit context.

READY, PREPARED
Thumbs of open hands (or just one hand) tap upper chest twice, or make upward brushing movements. Also means **GET READY.**

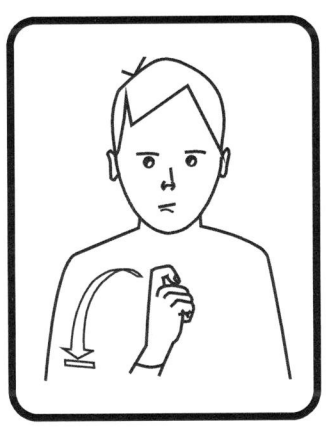

REDUNDANT, LAY OFF
Irish 'T' hand moves forward/down or in **direction** relevant to context.

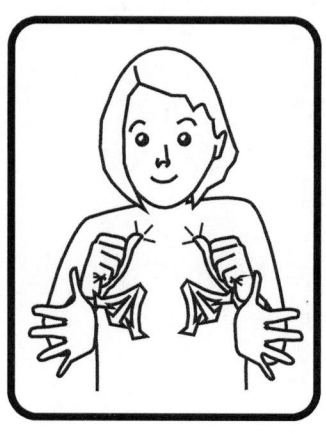

RETIRE, RETIREMENT
Thumb tips of closed hands contact chest, then hands spring forward/open.

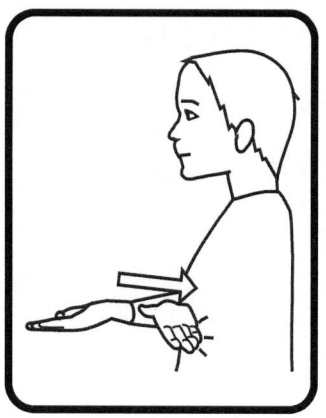

RIGHT, RIGHTS
Palm up flat hand moves back to touch lower chest. Used as in *'it's your right" 'what are my rights?'*

RISK/Y, APPREHENSIVE
Tips of 'O hand tap into neck twice, lips stretched with teeth clenched.

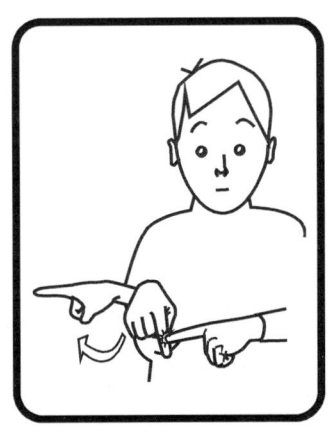

SACK, DISMISS, FIRE

R. index fingers twists sharply forward from wrist, brushing against tip of L. index finger. **Directional**.

SAFE, SAFETY, SECURE

R. bent hand on L. palm as hands move back to body.

SAME, SIMILAR, LIKE

Index fingers pointing forward contact each other. May tap twice or make single contact. Also means **ALSO, TOO**.

SCREEN, MONITOR, TV
Index fingers move out, down and inwards in outline shape of screen.

SEE YOU LATER
R. 'V' hand (or index finger) moves forward from eye, then index moves to the right in small arc.

SERVICE/S, PROVIDE
Palm up flat hands move together from the right to the front of body. Also means **PROVISION.**

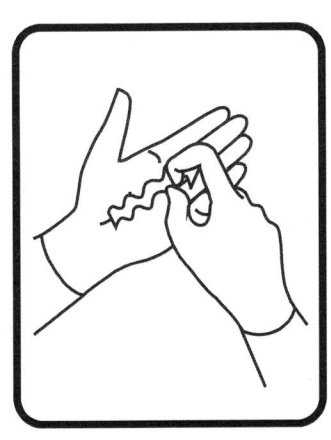

SIGN ON
'R' hand moves in writing action on L. palm. Also means to **SIGN, SIGNATURE.**

SIGN, SIGNING
Open hands move up and down alternately, or in alternate forward circles.

SIT DOWN, CHAIR, SEAT
Palm down closed hands make short firm movement down.

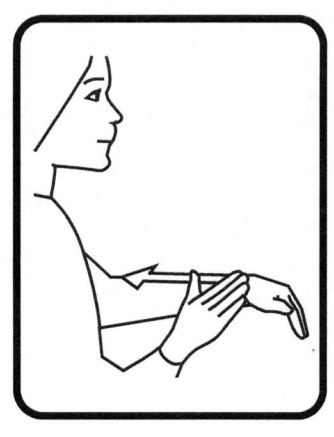

SLOW, SLOWLY, AGES
R. hand brushes from left wrist up the forearm. Also means **LONG TIME.**

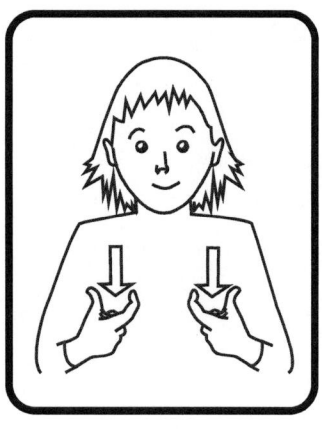

SOCIAL WORKER
Fingertips of 'C' hands move down sides of chest. May repeat. 'SW' or 'S worker' also sometimes used.

SORRY, REGRET
Closed hand rubs in circular movements on the chest with sorrowful expression. Little finger may be extended. ***Varies.***

STAIRS, GO UPSTAIRS
Fingers of bent 'V' hand wiggle in diagonal upwards movement.

START, BEGIN, COMMENCE
R. closed hand with thumb up moves sharply down behind L. flat hand. *Varies.*

STAY, REMAIN, BE STILL
Palm down 'C' hands (or one hand) make short firm movement down or in *direction* of referent.

STOP, WAIT, HOLD ON
Palm forward flat hand (or both hands) makes a short firm forward movement. Repeats for **WAIT, HOLD ON** etc. *Varies.*

STUDY, READ
Palm back flat hands move together side to side several times.

TEA, CAFE, CUP OF TEA
'O' hand moves up and tips slightly back to the mouth.

TELEPHONE, CALL
'Y' hand held near ear. May move forward eg '*I'll phone*' or onto chest eg '*call me*' (***directional***). See also **MOBILE PHONE.**

TEXT MESSAGE, SMS
Thumb flexes repeatedly as hand moves in small circles.

THANK YOU, APPRECIATE
Tips of flat hand touch mouth, then hand swings forward/down to finish palm up. Both hands can be used.

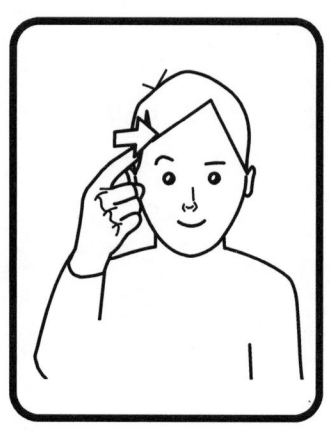

THINK

Index finger contacts side of forehead. May tap twice or make circular movements.

TICKET, CARD, PASS

Index fingers and thumbs extended and touching, move apart in outline shape. Also **RECEIPT, SLIP**. *Varies*.

TIME TO GO

R. index finger taps back of L. wrist **(TIME)**, then swings to point forward **(GO)**.

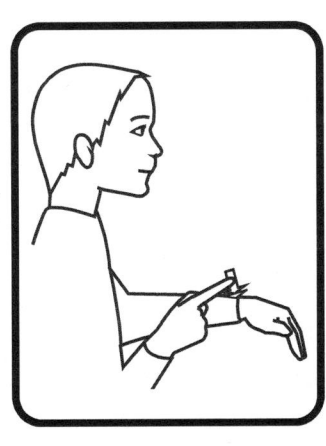

TIME, WHAT TIME?

R. index taps back of left wrist twice. With brows raised or furrowed means **WHAT TIME?**

TODAY, AT THE MOMENT

Palm up flat hands make two short movements down. Single firm movement for **AT ONCE.**

TOMORROW, NEXT DAY

Index finger on side of cheek twists forward/down from the wrist to finish palm up. With 'V' hand means **IN TWO DAYS.**

TRAIN, LEARN, STUDY
Tips of bunched hands together as hands move forward/down twice. Also means **STUDENT, TRAINEE**. *Varies.*

TRAIN, LEARN, STUDY
Palm down R. flat hand brushes forward against L. twice. Also means **STUDENT, TRAINEE**. *Varies.*

TRAIN, RAILWAY
Closed hand (or fist) makes firm forward movement at side of body, or forward circular movements.

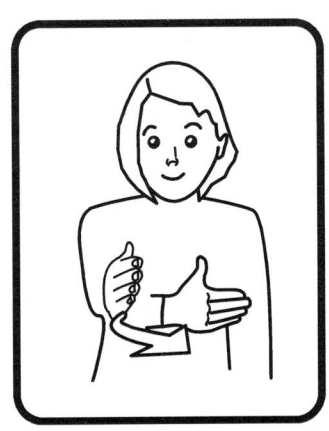

TURN LEFT

R. hand pointing forward swings to the left.

TURN RIGHT

R. hand pointing forward swings to the right.

TYPETALK, RELAY CALL

'Y' hands swap round to change places.

UNDERGROUND, TUBE
R. extended index finger moves forward under palm down L. flat hand.

UNEMPLOYED, NO WORK
R. flat hand chops down onto L. at right angles, then hands move apart, palm up with headshake. Also means **OUT OF WORK**.

UNION, STEWARD
Tips of bent 'V' hand and thumb tap left upper chest twice, or make small twisting movement. Also means **BADGE, BROOCH**.

USE, USEFUL

Fingers of bent hand and thumb on chin close to bunched hand twice. Also one version of **TEMPORARY.** *Varies*.

USE, USEFUL

Side of thumb brushes down twice off chin. Also *regional* **MAN.**

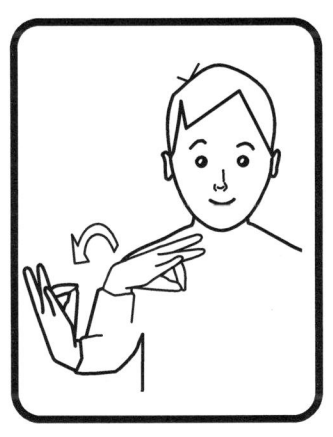

VOLUNTEER, INVITE/D

Tips of 'O' hand contact upper chest, then hand twists over and forwards, or tugs forward. Also means **BE CHOSEN, INVITATION.**

WAGE/S, PAY, SALARY

Fingers and thumb of R. bent hand close together as hand moves back down onto L. palm. R. clawed hand can be used.

WAIT

Closed hands palms forward/down make small inwards circles, or palm down bent hands make two short movements down.

WANT, NEED

Flat hand brushes down side of chest twisting to palm down.

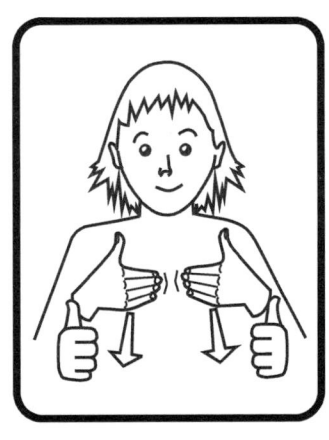

WELL, FINE, HEALTH
Bent hands touch chest then move forward closing with thumbs up. With raised brows means **ARE YOU WELL?**

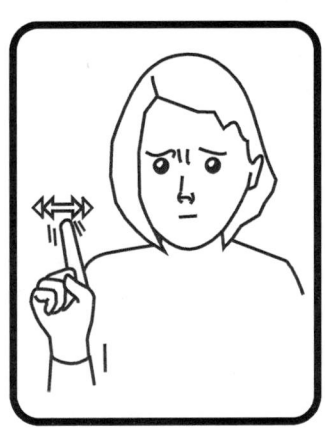

WHAT? WHAT FOR?
Palm forward index makes small side to side shaking movements, eyebrows raised or furrowed. Also *regional* **WHY?**

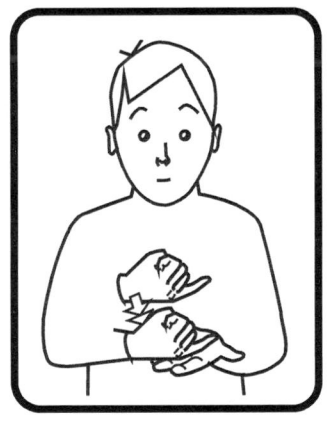

WHAT'S WRONG?
Extended little finger taps L. palm twice, eyebrows raised or furrowed. Also means **WHAT'S THE MATTER?**

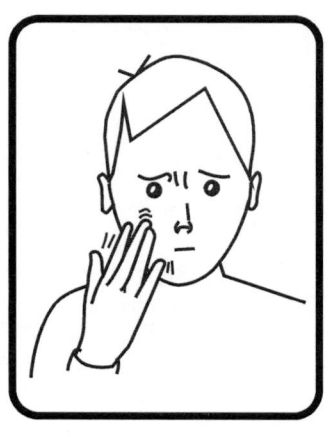

WHEN?
Fingers wiggle at side of face, eyebrows raised or furrowed.

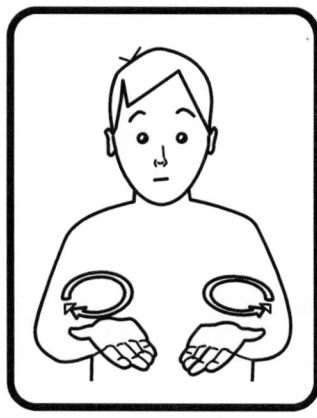

WHERE? WHEREABOUTS
Palm up hands move in small outward circles, or hands may move in-out towards each other, eyebrows raised or furrowed.

WHICH?
'Y' hand moves from side to side or between the objects or persons referred to, eyebrows raised or furrowed.

WHO?
Palm left R. index fingertip taps chin twice, eyebrows raised or furrowed. ***Varies.***

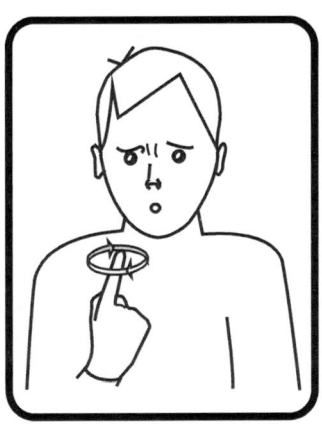

WHO?
Index finger makes small horizontal circles, eyebrows raised or furrowed. ***Varies.***

WHY?
Edge of R. index taps side of left upper chest twice, eyebrows raised or furrowed. Can also mean **BECAUSE** with neutral expression.

WORK, CAREER, JOB
Edge of R. flat hands makes short forward tapping movements on L. at right angles. Also means **EMPLOYMENT.**

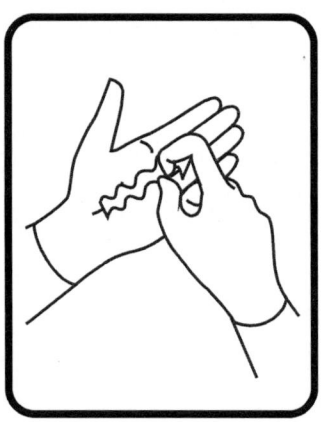

WRITE, PEN AND PAPER
R. 'O' hand moves along L. palm with squiggling movements. Also means **SIGN FOR, SIGN ON, TAKE NOTES.**

YESTERDAY, DAY BEFORE
Index finger on side of cheek twists back/down onto shoulder. With 'V' hand means **TWO DAYS AGO.**

YOU
Index points with short movement towards referent (with eye gaze). Sideways sweep for plural. ***Directional***.

YOUR, YOURS
Palm forward closed hand is directed towards referent (with eye gaze). Sideways sweep for plurals. ***Directional.***

YOURSELF, HIM/HERSELF
Palm back index held forward makes short movements down/forward in ***direction*** of referent.

RECOMMENDED RESOURCES AND READING

British Deaf Association (1992)
Dictionary of British Sign Language/English. London: Faber and Faber.

Klima, E. and Bellugi, U. (1979)
The Signs of Language. Harvard University Press.

Rachel Sutton-Spence and Bencie Woll (1999)
The Linguistics of British Sign Language: An Introduction. Cambridge University Press.

The LET'S SIGN Series (2001 - present)
BSL Educational Resources (See back of book) Co-Sign Communications (DeafBooks).
see page 4 for contact details.

NDCS (various publications)
National Deaf Children's Society
Ground Floor South, Castle House
37- 45 Paul Street
London EC2A 4LS
t: 020 7490 8656
e: ndcs@ndcs.org.uk
w: ndcs.org.uk

USEFUL CONTACTS

Organisations and Groups who work with DeafBooks and the Let's Sign Graphics

Down Syndrome Training & Support Service Ltd

Registered charity run by & for parents and carers of children who have Down Syndrome, offering support and training.

The Pamela Sunter Centre

2 Whitley Street, Bingley BD16 4JH
t: 01274 561308
e: office@downsyndromebradford.co.uk
w: www.downsyndromebradford.com

LET'S SIGN BSL - Co-Sign Communications (inc. DeafBooks)

For the Let's Sign BSL Series
Stockton-on-Tees, TS18 5HH
t: 01642 580505
e:info@letssign.co.uk - info@deafbooks.co.uk
w: LetsSign.co.uk - **w:** www.DeafBooks.co.uk

MeSign

British Sign Language Specialists.
The Office, The Robert Atkinson Centre, Thornaby, Stockton-On-Tees TS17 8AP
t: 07792010630
e: hello@mesign.co.uk
w: www.mesign.co.uk

National Deaf Children's Society (NDCS)

The leading charity for deaf children, for all deaf children no matter what their level or type of deafness or how they communicate.

Castle House, 37– 45 Paul Street, London
EC2A 4LS
t: 020 7490 8656
e: ndcs@ndcs.org.uk
w: www.ndcs.org.uk

The School Sign Shop

Beautifully designed School Signage Boards including a comprehensive range of BSL signs to encourage sign language comprehension amongst deaf and hearing children alike.

Unit 7 Moorswater Industrial Estate
Liskeard, Cornwall, PL14 4LN
t : 01579 340985
e: info@theschoolsignshop.co.uk
w: www.theschoolsignshop.co.uk

Royal Association for Deaf People (RAD)

RAD promote equality for Deaf people through the provision of accessible services.

t: 0845 688 2525 - **text phone:** 0845 688 2527
e: info@royaldeaf.org.uk
w: www.royaldeaf.org.uk

The Signing Company

Signs from British Sign Language (BSL) to teach signing to babies, children, families, educational practitioners and professionals.

e: enquiries@thesigningcompany.co.uk
w: www.thesigningcompany.co.uk

Widgit Software

Symbol Software & Let's Sign BSL graphics packs on licence.

1st Floor, Bishops House
Artemis Drive
Tachbrook Park
Warwick
CV34 6UD
t: 01926 333 680
e: info@widgit.com
w: www.widgit.com

USEFUL WEBSITES

www.signature.org.uk
www.spreadthesign.com
www.rnid.org.uk
www.signbsl.com
www.bslzone.co.uk

www.signworldlearn.com
www.bslsignbank.ucl.ac.uk
www.bbc.co.uk/seehear
www.ssc.education.ed.ac.uk
www.signdictionary.co.uk

INDEX

ABROAD	83	ASK	35
ACCESS	31	ASK	35
ACCIDENT.	77	ASSESS	36
ACQUIRE	72	ASSESS/MENT	36
ADDRESS	31	ASSESS/MENT	47
ADVICE	31	ASSISTANT	63
ADVISE/R	31	AT ONCE	99
AFTER	32	AT THE MOMENT	99
AFTER	32	ATTACH	70
AFTER	80	AUTHORITY	39
AFTERNOON	32	BAD	36
AFTERWARDS	32	BAD	36
AGAIN	33	BADGE	102
AGES	94	BE CHOSEN	103
AGREE	33	BE STILL	95
AGREEMENT	33	BECAUSE	107
ALARM	33	BECOME DEAF	62
ALRIGHT	34	BEFORE	36
ALSO	91	BEFORE	37
ALTER	43	BEFORE	81
ANTICIPATE	58	BEGIN	37
APPETISING	81	BEGIN	95
APPLY	35	BELL (clock, fire)	33
APPOINT	34	BENEFIT	67
APPOINTMENT	38	BESIDE	80
APPRECIATE	97	BEST	37
APPREHENSIVE	90	BISCUIT	38
APPROPRIATE	33	BISCUIT.	72
ARE	105	BOOK	38
ARE YOU OK?	34	BORE/D	39
ARE YOU WELL?	65	BORING	39
AREA	34	BOSS	53
ARISE	59	BOSS/Y	39
ARRIVE	35	BREAK	39

BRING	40	COMMUNICATE	45
BRING FORWARD	87	COMMUNICATION	45
BROOCH	102	COMMUNICATOR	45
BURN	57	COMPLETED	56
BUS	40	COMPULSORY	60
BUS	44	COMPUTER	45
BUSINESS	41	CONFERENCE	76
BUSY	41	CONFIDENTIAL	46
BUTT IN	31	CONNECT	46
BYE	41	CONNECTION	46
CAFE	96	CONSULT	79
CALL	97	CONTACT	46
CALLED	79	CONTINUE	46
CAR	42	CONTRACT	38
CAR PARK	42	CONVERSE	69
CARD	98	CONVERT	43
CAREER	108	CORRIDOR	47
CARRY ON	46	COURSE	47
CASH	78	COURT	47
CATALOGUE.	80	CROP UP	59
CELEBRATION	64	CRUCIAL	66
CERTIFICATE	42	CV	24
CHAIR	93	CUP OF TEA	96
CHANGE	43	DANGER	48
CHECK	43	DANGEROUS	48
CHECK OUT	60	DATE	82
CHEERIO	41	DAWN	48
CHIEF	53	DAY	48
CHIEF.	39	DAY BEFORE	108
CHOOSE	43	DEA DISABILITY EMPLOYMENT ADVISER	48
CLAIM	44		
CLOCK	33	DEA	24
COACH	44	DEAF	49
COFFEE	44	DEAF PERSON	49
COLLEGE	45	DEAFENED	62
COMMENCE	95	DEALINGS	79

115

DELAY	87
DEPART	72
DIALOGUE	69
DIFFERENCE	49
DIFFERENT	49
DIFFICULT/Y	60
DIRECT	49
DISABILITY	50
DISABLED	50
DISAGREE	50
DISAPPOINT	50
DISAPPOINT/MENT	50
DISCUSS	69
DISLIKE	51
DISMISS	91
DLA	24
DO	75
DOCTOR	51
DOLE	67
DON'T AGREE	50
DON'T KNOW	51
DON'T LIKE	51
DON'T NEED	52
DON'T WANT	52
DRIVE	40
DRIVE	42
DRIVER	40
DRIVER	42
EARLIER	36
EARLY	36
EARLY	52
EARNINGS	67
EASY	53
EAT	53
E-MAIL	52
EMERGENCY	52
EMPLOY	34
EMPLOYER	39
EMPLOYER	53
EMPLOYMENT	108
END	56
ENJOY	59
ENOUGH	55
ENQUIRY	70
ENROL	78
ENTER	67
ENTRY	67
ERROR	77
EVENING	54
EXPECT	58
EXPERIENCE	54
EXPLAIN	54
FAST	88
FAX	55
FED UP	55
FETCH	40
FILL IN FORM	55
FINANCE	78
FINE	34
FINE	105
FINGERSPELL	56
FINISH	56
FINISH/ED	56
FIRE	33
FIRE	57
FIRE	91
FIRE ESCAPE	57
FLAMES	57
FOOD	53
FOREIGN/ER	83
FORM	55
FREQUENTLY	33

FRESH	79	HEALTH AND SAFETY	61
FRUSTRATED	50	HEARING (not deaf)	61
GET	61	HEARING LOSS	62
GET BETTER	66	HELLO	58
GET READY	89	HELLO	62
GET TO	35	HELP/ER	63
GIFT	57	HERSELF	109
GIVE	57	HGV	24
GLAD	59	HGV	63
GLAD	86	HI	62
GO	58	HIMSELF	109
GO	72	HOLD ON	96
GO	98	HOLD ON	96
GO IN	67	HOLIDAY	63
GO THROUGH	31	HOLIDAY	64
GO UPSTAIRS	95	HOME	64
GOING TO	58	HOPE	64
GONE	58	HOPEFULLY	64
GOOD	58	HOUR	65
GOOD LUCK	75	HOW ARE YOU?	65
GOOD MORNING	78	HOW MANY?	82
GOODBYE	41	HOW OLD?	65
GREAT	58	HUMAN	85
GROUP	59	HURRY	88
HALL	47	HURT	68
HAPPEN	59	IDLE	72
HAPPY	59	ILL	66
HAPPY	86	ILLNESS	66
HARD	60	IMPORTANT	66
HARD OF HEARING	62	IMPROVE	66
HARD WORK	41	IMPROVEMENT	66
HAVE	61	IN	67
HAVE A LOOK	60	IN THE PAST	37
HAVE TO	60	IN TWO DAYS	99
HEAD	39	INCOME	67
HEALTH	105	INDOORS	67

117

INFORM	68	LET YOU KNOW	73
INFORMATION	68	LET'S SEE	60
INJURY	68	LETTER	73
INSIDE	67	LIGHT	48
INSURANCE	68	LIGHT (on)	74
INSURANCE	73	LIGHT (weight)	74
INSURE	68	LIKE	91
INTEND	58	LINK	46
INTERNET	69	LINK	70
INTERPRET/ER	69	LIVE	31
INTERRUPT	31	LOCAL	34
INTERVIEW	69	LONG TIME.	94
INTERVIEW	70	LOOK	75
INVITATION	103	LOOK AFTER	74
INVITE	43	LOOK AT	75
INVITE/D	103	LORRY	40
JOB	108	LOSE HEARING	62
JOIN	46	LUCK/Y	75
JOIN	70	LUNCH	53
KEYBOARD	45	MAGAZINE	80
KNOW	70	MAIL	73
KNOW ABOUT	54	MAKE	75
LAPTOP COMPUTER	71	MAKE A BOOKING	38
LATE	71	MAN	103
LATER	32	MANAGER	39
LATEST	79	MANAGER	53
LAW	71	MATHS	82
LAY OFF	89	MATTER?	105
LAZY	72	MAYBE	76
LEARN	72	MEDICAL	51
LEARN	100	MEET	76
LEARN	100	MEETING	76
LEAVE	72	MEND	75
LEISURE	39	MIGHT	76
LET	57	MINE, MY, MY OWN	77
LET ME KNOW	73	MISS	50

MISTAKE	77	OVERDUE	71
MOBILE PHONE	97	OWNER	53
MOBILE-PHONE	77	PAPER	83
MONEY	78	PARK	84
MONITOR	92	PARTIALLY DEAF	84
MORNING	78	PASS	98
MORTGAGE	85	PASSAGE	47
MUST	60	PAST	37
NAME	79	PAY	84
NAME DOWN	78	PAY	85
NEED	104	PAY	104
NEGOTIATE	79	PAY FOR	84
NET	69	PAYMENT	84
NEW	79	PAYMENTS	85
NEWSPAPER	80	PEN AND PAPER	108
NEXT	80	PENSION	67
NEXT DAY	99	PEOPLE	85
NEXT TO	80	PERHAPS	76
NICE	81	PERMANENT.	46
NIGHT	54	PERSONAL PAGER	86
NO WORK	102	PESTER	35
NOBODY	81	PICK	43
NONE	81	PLACE	34
NOT WELL	66	PLEASE	86
NOT YET	81	PLEASED	86
NOTES	55	POLICY	87
NOTHING	81	POSSESS/ION	61
NOW	82	POSTPONE	87
NUMBER	82	PREPARED	89
OFFER	57	PRESENT	57
OFFICE	82	PREVIOUS	37
OFFICE	83	PRINCIPLE	71
OFTEN.	33	PRINCIPLES	87
OK	34	PRIVATE	87
OUT OF WORK	102	PROFOUNDLY DEAF	49
OUTSIDE	83	PROVIDE	92

119

PROVISION	92	RIGHT NOW	82
PUBLIC	85	RIGHTS	90
PUT LIGHT ON	74	RISK/Y	90
PUT OFF	87	RULE	71
QUALIFICATION	42	RULES	87
QUALIFICATION/S	88	SACK	91
QUALIFIED	88	SAFE	91
QUALITY	88	SAFETY	91
QUERY	88	SALARY	104
QUESTION	88	SAME	91
QUICK	52	SCHEME	47
QUICK	88	SCREEN	45
RAILWAY	100	SCREEN	92
REACH	35	SEAT	93
READ	89	SECRET	87
READ	96	SECRETARY	83
READY	89	SECURE	91
REALLY DEAF	49	SEE	75
RECEIPT	98	SEE YOU LATER	92
REDUNDANT	89	SELECT	43
REGION.	34	SEND A FAX	55
REGRET	94	SENT	58
REGULATIONS	87	SERVICE/S	92
RELAX.	39	SICK OF	55
RELAY CALL	101	SIGN	93
REMAIN	95	SIGN	93
REMIND	35	SIGN FOR	78
RENT	85	SIGN FOR	108
REPAIR	75	SIGN ON	93
REPEAT	33	SIGN ON	108
REQUEST	35	SIGNATURE	93
RESERVE	38	SIGNING	93
REST	39	SIMILAR	91
RETIRE	90	SIMPLE	53
RETIREMENT	90	SIT DOWN	93
RIGHT	90	SLIP	98

SLOW	94	TELEPHONE	97
SLOWLY	94	TELL ABOUT	54
SMS	97	TEMPORARY.	103
SOCIAL WORKER	94	TEST	43
SOFT	53	TEXT MESSAGE	97
SORRY	77	TEXT PHONE	77
SORRY	94	THANK YOU	97
SPELL	56	THANKS	86
STAIRS	95	THEN	32
STAMP	73	THEN	80
START	37	THINK	98
START	95	TICKET	98
STATIONARY (car)	84	TIME	98
STAY	95	TIME	99
STEWARD	102	TIME TO GO	98
STOP	56	TIRED	66
STOP	96	TO BOOK	38
STRAIGHT	49	TODAY	99
STRAIGHT ON	49	TOILET	31
STUDENT	100	TOILET	24
STUDENT	100	TOMORROW	99
STUDY	96	TOO	91
STUDY	100	TOP	66
STUDY	100	TRADE	79
SUBSTITUTE	34	TRAIN	100
SUDDEN	52	TRAIN	100
SUIT/ABLE	33	TRAIN	100
SUPERVISE	74	TRAINEE	100
SUPPER	53	TRAINEE.	100
SUPPLY	34	TRIAL	47
SUPPORT	63	TRIBUNAL	47
SWEET	81	TRUCK	40
TAKE IN	72	TRY OUT	43
TAKE NOTES	108	TUBE	40
TEA	96	TUBE	102
TEAM	59	TURN	80

TURN LEFT	101
TURN RIGHT	101
TV	92
TV	24
TWO DAYS AGO	108
TYPE.	45
TYPETALK	101
UNDERGROUND	40
UNDERGROUND	102
UNEMPLOYED	102
UNION	102
URGENT	52
USE	103
USEFUL	103
VAN	40
VOLUNTEER	103
WAGE/S	104
WAGES	67
WAIT	81
WAIT	96
WAIT	96
WAIT	104
WANT	104
WEB	69
WELL	105
WENT	58
WHAT AGE?	65
WHAT FOR?	105
WHAT TIME?	99
WHAT?	105
WHAT'S THE	105
WHAT'S WRONG?	105
WHEN?	106
WHERE?	106
WHEREABOUTS	106
WHICH?	106
WHO?	107
WHY?	105
WHY?	107
WISH	64
WORK	108
WRITE	108
WRONG	36
WRONG	36
YAWN	39
YESTERDAY	108
YOU	109
YOU WELL?	105
YOUR	109
YOURS	109
YOURSELF	109

SERIES
British Sign Language (BSL) Resources

See our beautiful new school signage boards for playgronds and classrooms. Vibrant colours and designs in a wide choice of topics.

British Sign Language Educational Materials

BSL & SSE Graphics

Curriculum Support

Communication Inclusion

NEW Early Years Topic Books

Dictionaries, Posters, Flashcards, Kindles & Apps

www.DeafBooks.co.uk
BSL Resources & Free Downloads